A CLINICIAN'S GUIDE TO LEGAL ISSUES IN PSYCHOTHERAPY

—————— *Or* ——————

PROCEED WITH CAUTION

▪ A CLINICIAN'S GUIDE TO LEGAL ISSUES IN PSYCHOTHERAPY

OR

PROCEED WITH CAUTION

WILLIAM H. REID, M.D., M.P.H.

ZEIG, TUCKER & CO., INC.
PHOENIX, ARIZONA

Library of Congress Cataloging–in–Publication Data

Reid, William H., 1945-
    A clinician's guide to legal issues in psychotherapy, or, Proceed
with caution / William H. Reid.
        p. cm.
    Includes bibliographical references and index.
    Other title: Proceed with caution.
    ISBN 1-891944-08-8
    1. Psychologists—Legal status, laws, etc.—United States Popular
works. 2. Psychologists—Malpractice—United States Popular works.
3. Psychotherapists—Legal status, laws, etc.—United States Popular
works. 4. Psychotherapists—Malpractice—United States Popular
works. 5. Psychology—Moral and ethical aspects. 6. Psychotherapy—
Moral and ethical aspects. I. Title. II. Title: Proceed with
caution.
    [DNLM: WM 420 R359c 1999]
KF2910.P75R45   1999
344.73'04121—dc21
DNLM/DLC
for Library of Congress   99–19558
                                                                      CIP

Published by

Zeig, Tucker & Co., Inc.
3618 North 24 Street
Phoenix, Arizona 85016

Manufactured in the United States of America

10 9 8 7 6 5 4 3 2 1

To those who put patients first,
and who struggle and speak out against those who don't,

and to Elise.

Contents

INTRODUCTION   1

1. FIRST, PRACTICE WELL   5
2. A BRIEF LOOK AT THE LAW   15
3. ADHERING TO CLINICAL STANDARDS OF CARE   31
4. PROFESSIONAL RELATIONSHIPS   43
5. RELATIONSHIPS WITH PATIENTS AND FAMILIES   58
6. PRACTICE SETTINGS AND STYLES   69
7. CONSENT   75
8. BOUNDARY VIOLATIONS   80
9. CONFIDENTIALITY AND PRIVILEGE   91
10. SUICIDE AND OTHER DANGER TO SELF   99
11. WHEN THERE IS DANGER TO OTHERS   108
12. DEALING WITH IMPAIRED OR UNETHICAL COLLEAGUES   121
13. ADVERSE AND SIDE EFFECTS OF TREATMENT   129
14. FORENSIC TRAINING AND PRACTICE   133
15. ON BEING SUED   139

APPENDIXES

A. Results of the 1997-1998 Reid/Zeig, Tucker National
Survey on Forensic Issues in the Mental Health Professions   147

B.   Forms Used in Clinical and Forsenic Practice   155

C.   Glossary of Common Legal and Forensic Terms   167

D.   Further Resources   186

      Index   189

A Clinician's Guide to Legal Issues in Psychotherapy

─────── *Or* ───────

Proceed with Caution

INTRODUCTION

Y OU DON'T WANT to see me, or someone like me, across the room
from you at a trial or deposition—which is not a bad reason to read
this book.

A Clinican's Guide to Legal Issues in Psychotherapy is about lowering
your legal risks in individual clinical practice, including understanding
common forensic issues and standards as they apply to mental health
professionals, recognizing potential problems, and clarifying the
risk–benefit issues involved in what you are doing. It is *not* about how
to avoid trouble if you are doing something you already know is bad, nor
is it about watering down your clinical approach simply to mollify
unreasonable critics, lawyers, or insurers.

The old saying about quality practice protecting you from lawsuits
still has merit, and good, ethical practice, putting patients first, goes a
long way toward such protection. On the other hand, anyone can sue
you, for almost any reason. Anyone can file a complaint with your
licensing board or certifying body. Anyone can make your life miserable,
whether or not you are eventually "exonerated." It is thus important to try
to stop problems before they start, and to know something about the
law's way of handling those that do arise. You practice good care, so
document it. You usually know "the right thing to do" when faced with
ethical quandaries, so do it. You know how to check your colleagues'
credentials and reputations, so don't associate with people or organizations that are likely to get you—and patients—into trouble.

I am not a lawyer. I thought about inviting a lawyer to coauthor this
book and so try to cover the legal waterfront, but decided to keep it simple. The law, unlike the ethics and principles that often underlie it, is
fluid. Social and political conditions cause frequent changes that can
take clinicians by surprise. Some are easy to keep up with, such as state
practice rules or prohibitions; others, such as malpractice case law and

precedents for proving negligence, are obscure until you suddenly meet up with them (e.g., in court). For more detailed information, see the resources listed in Appendix D (or, if you are really worried, get to know a competent lawyer who specializes in mental health). *Do not* construe this book as legal advice! It isn't.

This book was written specifically for nonphysician mental health practitioners, including psychologists, psychotherapists, and counselors. Although it does not focus on material directly related to biological treatments, biological diagnosis, and the like, it does address many issues encountered by psychiatrists and professionals who work in medical settings or with physician colleagues. The material comes largely from my own experience at the interface of mental health and the law. Much of the topic emphasis is from *you*: your responses to our 1997–98 national survey on forensic issues in the mental health professions.

You will find that I prefer the word "patient" to "client" or (God forbid) "consumer" or "recipient" (as actually used in the Illinois public mental health system). I am aware of the need to treat the people whom we are trying to help with respect, and of the damage that unfair stigma can do to recovery and self-esteem. Nevertheless, I quietly campaign for "patient" for a number of reasons. First, "patients" have a specific place in the public mind, a place that is different from that of a "client" or "consumer," and that associates the person with deserving a certain standard of care and treatment. Second, people take patient status much more seriously than they do client or consumer status, and we need to be more serious about mental health and mental illness. Third, *legislatures* and *payers* take the concept of patient more seriously, for purposes of funding treatment and research. Fourth, the term "patient" is harder to trivialize than are the other terms. It is grossly unfair to drive a semantic wedge between the mentally ill and other patients, and thus to imply that people with depression, schizophrenia, or panic disorder merely need good information or advocacy from their clinicians.

A senior Cabinet advisor who has bipolar disorder spoke to leaders of the American Psychiatric Association a few years ago. He said, in part, that he does not want to be called a "client" or "consumer," but a *patient*. He wants legislators and insurers to refer to his condition as a *mental illness*, not a "behavioral health" problem. The reason he gave was simple: If these terms are not used, his condition (and those of thousands of other patients) becomes trivialized compared with other medical disorders, and funding for treatment and research becomes much harder to get.

A word about the risk of lawsuits, and of losing assets in damage judgments: In the world of plaintiffs' attorneys, the primary difference between types of clinicians is the level of assets vulnerable to lawsuits (e.g., individual malpractice coverage, employer assets or insurance). When the litigation target is an organization, the principle of *respondeat superior* (Chapter 2) suggests that lower-level counselors will be criticized as often as are clinical psychologists and psychiatrists. When the clinician is an independent therapist, however, the expense of plaintiff litigation dictates that those with more vulnerable assets (usually in the form of malpractice insurance) are sued more often than are those with fewer assets. Note, however, that some individual therapists are affiliated with, but often not employed by, larger organizations, which may make plaintiffs' litigation worthwhile. The point of avoiding suit is not only how much money one stands to lose, but the considerable problems involved in being a defendant.

I have been a clinician, teacher, writer, and researcher for many years, and now devote most of my time to working at that interface, reviewing and evaluating cases, assessing litigants, advising courts and attorneys, and sometimes testifying in court or at deposition. Astute readers will note that I am a psychiatrist; nevertheless, my forensic work involves individual mental health professionals and practice settings of all kinds. In civil cases (such as malpractice or other lawsuits), I am sometimes retained by the plaintiff, sometimes by the defense, and sometimes by the Court itself. What you will find in these pages is designed to keep you from having unwanted contact with people like me, and to provide information that may help if you do.

William H. Reid, M.D., M.P.H.

■ 1

First, Practice Well

It is a truism that good clinical practice decreases one's likelihood of being the target of outside criticism or lawsuit, simply because it increases the opportunity for good outcome, positive patient relationships, and peer respect. In addition, good practice, almost by definition, keeps one within the standard of care and clinical duty. The world isn't fair, of course, and bad outcomes, problems with difficult or litigious patients and families, misunderstandings, and honest mistakes do occur. Nevertheless, one's effort to work competently and diligently goes a long way toward preventing tragedy, misunderstanding, and/or accusations of malpractice.

Be Well Trained and Credentialed

Mental health professionals know that psychotherapy is not just, as Thomas Szasz once said to the author, "schmoozing with patients." The profession has little place for those who call themselves therapists or counselors solely by virtue of their interest in helping people or some misguided wish for the title. This book is designed to help therapists and other professionals who have completed legitimate graduate training programs, have become appropriately licensed, have had supervised experience, and have maintained their skills through continuing education and consultation. Those who do not meet these criteria should, at the least, (1) avoid overestimating or misrepresenting their qualifications and (2) recognize (and be prepared for) patients who need referral for professional care.

KNOW YOUR PROFESSIONAL AND EMOTIONAL "WEAK SPOTS," AND WHEN THEY'RE BEING TESTED

Knowing the limits of one's training and experience is basic to practicing well: its value is widely recognized and need not be emphasized here. Some therapists, particularly those with little psychodynamic background or personal therapy, may not realize that awareness of countertransference vulnerabilities is just as basic.

"Countertransference" is a subset of that which we might call "emotional vulnerability." I'm not speaking here of antisocial or exploitive therapists, but of those who sometimes work in good faith, then get into trouble because they don't recognize, and later have difficulty *controlling*, their own needs and impulses. Some very serious problems, such as blatant boundary violations (more about that in later chapters), can arise from good-faith caring coupled with inadequate training, recognition, management, and control of one's own needs and defenses.

Personal therapy, supervision, and case consultation all help, but sometimes require painful efforts to be professionally honest.

A senior, married, female post/doctoral trainee wanted supervised experience in the psychodynamic psychotherapy of antisocial patients. After discussing the need for close supervision and the likelihood of problems in the therapy, the program referred a man with a history of antisocial (including criminal) behavior. The trainee saw the patient twice a week and regularly attended her weekly supervision appointments with an analytically oriented psychiatrist known for his work with such patients.

After a few months of supervision, which included review of the therapy notes and management of occasional setbacks, the supervisor commented that the treatment had seemed unusually uneventful for a while. The next week, the trainee tearfully admitted that she had not been forthcoming with her feelings in the supervision, and that those feelings had led to what she described as her sexual seduction during a recent session. She was extremely ashamed and was now being physically threatened and the victim of extortion by the patient. It may be noted that the trainee had no apparent unethical intent and that the patient was not particularly physically attractive.

UNDERSTAND ETHICAL GUIDELINES—AND MORAL ONES

The foregoing vignette is not designed to illustrate an ethical dilemma, but one of countertransference and immaturity. Ethical matters are much clearer, whether or not one adheres to the ethical standard. Very few professionals who behave unethically are so asocial that they do not know the difference between right and wrong; those who do get no sympathy from the author, although they are welcome to read further about the possible consequences of their actions.

The problem arises (1) when some part of the therapist fuels a decision to go against that which he or she knows is right and (2) when "shades of gray" or "situational ethics" make it seem as though there is a dilemma when the choice is actually quite clear. Written ethical guidelines, such as those promulgated by the American Psychological Association, the National Association of Social Workers, and the American Psychiatric Association, remind us of specific canons, and often help to settle dilemmas in which two or more ethics concepts appear to conflict.

Of course, clarity is not always possible; however, the therapist should be certain that the ethical "dilemma" is not really just a choice between what is proper and what he or she simply *wishes* were proper. An institutional example of such pragmatic (or wishful) thinking comes from professionals and nonprofessionals who would have one believe that special clinical environments or issues—such as managed care, technological advances, or social exigencies—are reason to change our ethical underpinnings. It simply isn't so, and one follows them at some peril to self and patients.

A word about morals in psychotherapy. I like them. Our purpose is not the same as that of radio advisors like Dr. Laura Schlessinger (who regularly points out that her advice is not "therapy"), but we would do well to heed her plea for less "if-it-works-for-you-it's-O.K." feel-good psychobabble. Sometimes good therapists *do* help patients decide what's right, and even when directive comments are clinically inappropriate, it is difficult to think of a situation in which one should even passively support the part of the patient that wants to do bad things. Philosphical issues aside, therapists may be sued for such things as encouraging infidelity, contributing to divorce or family strife, and failing to recognize or intervene in dangerous or illegal activity.

CONTINUING EDUCATION, SUPERVISION, AND CONSULTATION

Professional organizations and licensing bodies recognize the importance of maintaining and updating clinical skills, as well as of learning about new developments (and laws) that affect one's patients and practice. Even very experienced therapists and other clinicians are rightly criticized if their patient care is limited by outdated information.

In addition to their educational value, continuing education and supervision offer a chance to compare one's skills and abilities with the current standard, and sometimes to recognize more serious deficits (see below). Clinicians have a duty to be aware of their own limitations and shortcomings and to protect patients from any incompetence or significant impairment they may have.

"Supervision" (unlike "consultation," see below) implies an ongoing relationship with a colleague, often an academic or professional superior, which carries either a mandate or a strong suggestion that the supervisor's recommendations will be followed in some way. Good clinicians know that supervision and consultation are not just for trainees. The nature of our work requires current skills and knowledge, and continuous monitoring of the interface between the patient's needs and our own impulses and defenses. It is not unusual for therapists to contract with a peer or senior colleague to act as a private, ongoing consultant in one case or several.

Such a relationship may be disclosed to patients (and should be if the therapist is in training or has some formal requirement for supervision, such as a licensure problem), although it need not be under some circumstances. Private, nonmandatory supervision may be seen as "consultation," and may not generate a mandate to follow the supervisor's recommendations. Many other forms of supervision do include such a mandate, although the method for following the advice may or may not be specifically prescribed.

Supervision, as used here, is not the same as "co-treatment" or "divided treatment," in which two cooperating clinicians provide different services to the patient (e.g., medication from a psychiatrist and cognitive-behavioral therapy from a psychologist, or conjoint therapy from a family therapist and individual counseling for a family member from a clinical social worker). Since the word "supervision" may have legal overtones, it is best not to confuse it with co-treatment in documentation or conversation, and to clarify the parameters of the relationship in a written note.

"Consultation" is generally a brief, advisory event that does not generate any mandate to act as the consultant may suggest. Nevertheless, the therapist has a duty to consider the consultant's findings and to make reasonable decisions considering that added information. The potential for criticism or litigation in complex cases is one (but not the main) reason to seek consultation. The presence of qualified consultation adds greatly to the therapist's defense in case of a tragedy, although this is not usually the only reason for seeking it. In the words of Dr. Thomas Gutheil, speaking of risk management for clinicians in difficult situations: "Never worry alone."

Part of the point of this section is to encourage therapists not to practice in isolation. Even in small towns, there is almost always an opportunity (by computer or telephone at the least) to interact with other professionals, test and monitor one's skills, and consult with experienced colleagues.

Intellectual and professional isolation is a larger problem. Even in urban settings, therapists should be alert to the temptation to think of their work as unique or special, something only they can do and to which other professionals cannot really contribute. Sometimes the temptation extends to avoiding continuing education in any but one's narrow field of interest, or avoiding it altogether. Such feelings often overlay fears of being found incompetent or unacceptable by peers, sometimes in clinicians who think their rusty skills will embarrass them if they seek supervision or additional training. They can lead to defensively overestimating one's own skills, avoiding needed consultations, and inviting boundary problems. Don't go there.

Know the Parameters of Co-treatment ("Divided Treatment")

Sharing treatment with a colleague of a different specialty offers the patient more than your own expertise (and perhaps your time or patient obligation, as in a conflict with a duty to an individual patient's interest) can provide. On the other hand, such co-treatment ("divided treatment"), even though not supervisory or consultative in the sense described above, *does not* diminish your standard of care or general exposure to liability, and almost always adds to it.

You are obligated to know the qualifications of those with whom you work or to whom you refer patients, and to communicate with them as clinically necessary in the interest of the patient (at the least keeping them informed of progress, treatment changes, or problems). In some cases, a local standard or guideline may imply that you have some responsibility for the overall care of the patient, regardless of who provides it (e.g., in the case of a psychiatrist or other physician who provides a diagnosis and prescribes psychotropic medication but refers "his" or "her" patient elsewhere for psychotherapy). Various ways in which joint liability may arise or be modified are discussed in Chapter 4.

Don't Let the Patient Dictate Bad Treatment

After all is said and done, you—not the patient—are the clinician. Some therapists and counselors go much too far, for a variety of reasons, to try to give the patient what he or she wants while shortchanging (or even ignoring) what is therapeutically correct. Starting and staying on the most "therapeutic" course is harder when the therapist is inexperienced and not confident in his or her skills; when the patient is quite assertive (or subtly threatening, such as implying that he or she may leave or not pay the bill); when the patient is seductive (not necessarily sexually) or other conscious or countertransference opportunities (such as anger, narcissism, or disgust) affect the clinician's judgment; when the patient's need is outside one's expertise but the request is not; and when the patient is unusual in some way (e.g., a professional, a "VIP," or one who has a particularly interesting diagnosis).

There is often a difference between patient acceptance of treatment and "consent" (discussed in Chapter 7). Clinicians need the patient's consent (expressed or implied, as pertinent); however, the therapist must agree that the treatment is appropriate in the first place. To act otherwise is at best a waste of time and resources, and at worst a dereliction of one's duty to provide (or refer the patient for) treatment that meets the standard of care.

You aren't the patient's friend. Friends often do what we want them to, and try to please us and keep us in their lives. Friend*liness*, respect, compassion, courtesy, and empathy are all important to quality care, but the patient needs your skills and competence much more than your friendship. When therapy and friendship are combined, there is a danger that the treatment will be severely compromised. You should act in the patient's interest, but you must understand that interest as a clinical one, and not as a social or personal one. The patient has a right to expect that you will be a competent, objective professional.

PROVIDE THE TIME

Attention to the patient's needs also involves a commitment of time and energy. The therapist need not—and should not, in most cases—stretch personal boundaries by extending session times or giving a home telephone number; nevertheless, one should convey availability appropriate to the therapeutic method and goals (which will be quite different for different kinds of patients and therapists), and not coldly shirk opportunities for, for example, simple courtesy or family contact. This is especially important during and after a crisis or tragedy.

Do not accept unreasonable time constraints in, for example, managed-care assessment or treatment settings. Your first responsibility, legal and ethical, is to the patient.

Document, Document, Document

Whoever started the rumor in professional circles that "if you don't write it down, they can't hang you with it" was dead wrong. In far more cases than not, complete, legible notes help clinicians whose care is questioned. Skimpy notes imply skimpy care. Merely saying that something important, like suicidal ideation, was "discussed" leaves juries with much more doubt about the discussion than confidence in its completeness. If you are sued, you will have a chance to explain your notes, but lawyers, judges, and juries place much more credence on what you wrote during treatment (known as "contemporaneous" notes) than on what you say later when your reputation, career, and money are on the line.

Similarly, write or dictate your notes within an hour or so of the activity they describe. It is easy to forget things that happened days or weeks before, and thus tempting to make the note shorter. Testing reports, as well as hospital assessments, treatment plans, discharge summaries, and the like, are commonly delayed, but delays that seem routine to other professionals look like sloppy care to judges and juries. It is especially embarrassing, and potentially incriminating, to have to prepare overdue reports, summaries, or other notes after a suicide or other tragedy has already occurred (and then try to convince a court that your words are not self-serving).

Write legibly, and be sure to place the patient's name and the complete current date (including the year) on each sheet of notes. In reviewing unbound copies a couple of years later, people who may be trying to help you need to understand the proper order of the pages.

If you keep your notes on a computer diskette or hard drive, be certain that there is a signed hard copy in the record as well. Files dated contemporaneously can easily be altered, and the court knows it. More often, all the notes are in one computer file with only the most recent file-alteration date—not very convincing if you are trying to show that part of the record was written months before.

Do not change your notes after the fact except by adding *and dating* additional or explanatory information, or flagging inaccuracies by drawing a line through them. There is no law (that I know of) against actually deleting inaccurate outpatient material, but it looks much better to acknowledge the error contemporaneously and to leave it semivisible in the record. All changes should be initialed and dated. Deleting or altering material to hide liability or criminal activity may well be a crime in itself.

Your records[1] must be disclosed under any of three conditions (and others, depending on the situation): (1) valid release by the patient, (2) legal cases in which the patient or a qualified substitute brings his or her care into question, and (3) legal cases brought by the patient or a qualified substitute in which mental health records may be relevant to the outcome. The first two are easy: Check with your lawyer to make sure that the request is valid, and if it is, provide all the records.

Therapists may balk at the third condition, perhaps because they don't see the relevance of their records to the legal case, and occasionally a judge must rule on the relevance. Nevertheless, whether or not to release once a lawful subpoena or other valid authorization has been received *is not up to you*. Incidentally, not all subpoenas are as "lawful" as they appear; if you are in doubt, check with your own lawyer.

The primary purpose of clinical notes is communication, both to other clinicians and to yourself as you treat the patient over time. Documentation for legal or defensive reasons is secondary, but important when one is trying to reconstruct past events. Accurate reconstruction is more likely to help you than harm you.

Know How to Get Along with Patients' Families

The patient and treatment don't exist in a vacuum. Many clinical situations benefit from (and some require) family contact of some sort. Complaints or litigation may arise from misunderstandings by family members, their lack of information about significant clinical events, their effect on treatment compliance and outcome, and/or failure of the therapist to seek important information from them when appropriate. If

---

[1] If you keep two different sets of notes, such as for a main clinic chart and your own use, *both* sets are discoverable. Therapist confidentiality is not as binding as that of priests and lawyers (see Chapter 9 on confidentiality and privilege).

a tragedy does occur, family communication—but not misplaced guilt or defensiveness—is important for all concerned (see Chapter 10).

Working While Impaired

The law and the standard of care have little sympathy for clinicians who knowingly work while physically or mentally impaired. "Knowingly," in this instance, includes knowing that one has a substance-abuse problem, a significant mental illness, a need to take medication to remain competent, or some other impairment reasonably expected to interfere with adequate care.

Every U.S. state (and many professional societies) has a mechanism for helping impaired therapists and clinicians to retain their licenses and practice safely and competently. When one complies with those mechanisms—separate from treatment or recovery programs, which may also be required—the probability of continuing practice is greatly enhanced and that of patient harm greatly diminished.

Your Reputation

"Who steals my purse steals trash . . . (b)ut he that filches from me my good name robs me of that which not enriches him, and makes me poor indeed." Shakespeare (*Othello* III, iii) was never more accurate.

·2

A Brief Look at the Law

Time for another I-am-not-a-lawyer disclaimer—but the information in this chapter is as reliable as I can make it.

Overview of the U.S. Legal System

Let's take a few paragraphs to explain the entire U.S. system of jurisprudence.

Permissive, Not Restrictive

In general, U.S. citizens do not have to ask permission to do things. Instead, they can do what they wish, provided there is no prior restriction. In other words, if there's no law against something, it's usually O.K. to do it. That distinction is important, and it is absent in many other countries (in which you can only do things that are "allowed"). In the absence of a "No Trespassing" notice, we can walk where we like. If there is no law against doing therapy in a fake nose and funny glasses, have at it.

Thus clinicians are free to be flexible in their approaches unless specifically limited by a law or other restriction. One doesn't have to do cognitive therapy as a matter of law (but see "standards" and "duty," below), no matter how many studies say it works and it's cost-effective.

Similarly, in the absence of a legal order to the contrary, people are free to take our treatment or leave it, as they choose.

In general, there are three ways in which the law can restrict citizens, including therapists. First, the U.S. Constitution and state constitutions establish basic rights and laws for the entire country and individual states respectively. Second, federal, state, and local governments can make laws (subject to the U.S. Constitution and—for nonfederal laws—relevant state constitutions). Third, and a subset of number two, government agencies may be empowered to make rules that have the force of law (such as the Health Care Financing Administration [HCFA] Medicare rules, licensing requirements, and state or local "administrative rules"). These are subservient to the U.S. *and* state constitutions *and* to laws passed by state and federal legislatures.

Jurisdiction

Most laws affect only small parts of the United States (and activities that take place in those parts). Administrative rules affect only those settings and locations for which they are specifically intended (e.g., the conduct of the ring physician during a New York prizefight). Parking laws in Dallas have no effect on where one can legally park in Chicago. State laws and state constitutional matters (such as state-generated rights) affect only the state in which they were passed. Federal laws and U.S. Constitutional matters affect everyone in the United States, its territories, U.S. military bases and embassies abroad, and the like. The state constitutions supersede state statutes (laws passed by state legislatures or assemblies); the U.S. Constitution supersedes federal statute, state constitutions and statutes, and your mother's advice.

The same jurisdictional concepts apply to trials and court findings. Local courts are subservient to state courts, which are subservient to state appeals courts, which are subservient to the state supreme court. Matters that involve federal (not state) law are heard in federal (not state) district courts, each of which is subservient to its related federal appeals court, which is subservient to the U.S. Supreme Court. Note that *all* state courts are subservient to the federal court in that geographic area, but that only federal matters or matters appealed from state supreme courts are tried in federal courts.

All of this means that the well-known *Tarasoff* decision, for example, which focused therapists' attention on duties to warn or protect potential victims of patient violence, is *legally relevant* only in California, since all of the decisions were made in state (not federal) courts (the case was finally decided in the Californian supreme court, not the U.S. Supreme Court). There is no nationwide legal "duty to warn"; it is a state-by-state matter.

Adversarial System

We often speak of the "adversarial system." This means that our courts seek the truth by having the two sides fight, with extensive rules that try to ensure a fair fight. In a way, the system expects that in a fair fight, the truth will triumph.

Burden of Proof

The system is designed to be "fair," but not "even." The U.S. Constitution considers the stakes in *criminal* matters, in which losing may mean losing one's liberty, to be so high that a very heavy burden of proving the case is placed on the prosecution (the "state" or "government"): every element of the criminal case must be proved beyond a reasonable doubt (something like 95–98% certainty). Thus, 19 or more guilty people should go free for every innocent one incarcerated.

In *civil* (noncriminal) matters, liberty is generally not at stake. The law's objective in lawsuits, for example (one kind of civil matter), is to force a culpable party to make the damaged party "whole" again. The prototypical way to make the damaged party "whole" is with money, and since only money, not liberty, is at stake, the plaintiff's burden of proof is much less: merely to show all the elements of liability to a more-likely-than-not level (just over 50% certainty).

A very few civil matters are considered to involve more than "mere money," and thus to require an intermediate level of proof ("clear and convincing proof," or about 75–80% certainty). Civil commitment, for example, removes a patient's liberty, but the patient gets something positive in return (needed care and/or treatment). Child-custody matters involve more than money as well, but have a similarly positive purpose (the best interests of the child). Both examples require more than a pre-ponderance of evidence to prove the petitioner's case, since the issues are more than mere money; however, neither uses deprivation of liber-ty as a punishment or intends negative consequences for the recipient, and thus does not require proof "beyond a reasonable doubt." (That is, it is not required as a matter of U.S. Constitutional protections. States may enact greater-than-constitutional protections; one or two states require proof beyond a reasonable doubt for civil commitment.)

As a Matter of Fact

"Facts" in legal parlance are not the same as "facts" in the ordinary world. It is sometimes important for therapists and other clinicians to know (when testifying, for example) that something may be described as a "fact" without having been proved. One should listen for such modifiers as "accepted," "agreed-upon," or "finding of" in order to understand what a lawyer means.

A "fact witness" in a legal case is one who is allowed to report only that which he or she knows from some kind of direct experience. One can thus tell what one saw, heard (as in "I heard two loud noises," but not secondhand conversations), or did oneself. A therapist may describe his or her diagnosis, therapy activities, and the outcome. Fact witnesses are not allowed to give opinions, such as "expert opinions."

This is important when therapists are called to testify about current or former patients. Unless you have been "qualified" by the court in that particular trial or legal action to testify as an expert, it is inappro-priate for you to give opinions or to testify to anything except your direct experience (although lawyers may ask about such things, and the court may or may not allow you to answer). Interestingly, every citizen has a duty to give fact testimony if asked (e.g., subpoenaed). You can't legally decline without a good reason (patient privilege/con-fidentiality may or may not be a good reason; see Chapter 9), and no one is obligated to pay you more than a few dollars (although lawyers who want you to testify often will offer to reimburse you for your time, since they want you to be in a good mood). Since expert witnesses have a duty to be objective but treating therapists have a duty to act in their patients' best interest, *testifying as an expert witness in a patient's* or *former patient's case usually involves a conflict of interest, and may be unethical.*

The "trier of fact" in a trial is the person or persons who decide(s) whether or not the evidence supports the petitioner's claim. The trier of fact may be a jury or a judge. There is also a "trier of law," always the judge, in every trial. The trier of law (judge) makes sure that the laws promoting trial fairness are followed (ruling on objections, whether or not to admit evidence, and generally controlling what the jury is allowed to see and hear). The trier of law (judge) may, on rare occasions, over-rule the trier of fact if he or she believes the case is legally (not factually) insufficient (but the judge may not overrule a jury's "not guilty" verdict in a criminal trial). All *appeals* of trial court verdicts must be based on matters of law, not fact; the fact issues stop with the trial (lower) court. Appellate and supreme courts listen to presentations by the attorneys on points of law; they do not hear testimony from witnesses.

MENTAL ILLNESS AND CRIMINAL LAW

Since this book is designed to help you avoid legal problems, not par-ticipate in them, we will only briefly address four issues in criminal law: competence, criminal responsibility, patients who are involved in the criminal justice system, and patients in the correctional system.

Clinicians doing assessments for the legal system must understand that its vocabulary and purpose are quite different from those of ordinary practice. The person being assessed is rarely one's "patient," and should be described instead as an "evaluee" or "defendant." Such words as "insanity" are important to the criminal court, even though they are no longer used in clinical settings. More important, the evaluating profes-sional must understand that the law has very specific definitions of "insanity," "competence," and other terms that may be quite different from their clinical or intuitive meanings. In order to be useful and under-stood by the court, one must know and use *its* definitions.

Competence, or competency, in criminal matters usually refers to a person's eligibility to stand trial, be sentenced, or have a sentence (especially a death sentence) carried out. In such cases, competence always refers to *current* competence to do something very specific (such as to understand the basic trial process or to cooperate with one's lawyer). Competence to stand trial has little or nothing to do with the person's condition at the time of the alleged criminal act (see below).

The concept of competence to stand trial arises from the constitutional requirement that defendants have the opportunity to be present at their trials, to defend themselves, and to confront the witnesses against them. Physical presence is not enough; mental presence is also required, and defendants who are mentally unable truly to "be there," to understand the rudiments of the process, to confront witnesses (e.g., by working through an attorney), and so on, cannot be tried. Persons found incompetent to stand trial are often sent to a secure hospital in the hope that they will regain competence. If they cannot do so within a reasonable period, then they must either be released or, if they meet civil commitment criteria, involuntarily hospitalized.

Similarly, persons who for some reason have been tried and then have lost competence (by the court's definition, not the doctor's) may have sentencing delayed or may be sent to an appropriate nonprison institution, depending on the applicable law. Those sentenced to death who lose competence to be executed may have the execution delayed or, if the incompetence is permanent, have their sentence changed.

Most clinical organizations consider it unethical to treat a person for the sole purpose of making him or her competent for execution. It is, however, ethically permissible to alleviate symptoms for other reasons (such as the inmate's discomfort or to prevent decompensation). The same organizations generally relax the ethical guidelines when the clinician is treating a patient in order to render him or her competent for other sentencing or trial, although individual professionals may, in some cases, consider it to be acting counter to the patient's interests.

Criminal Responsibility

In the United States, as in most cultures, a "criminal" act is not criminal unless it involves both a physical action (*actus rea*) and the mental intent to do something wrong (*mens rea*). Thus there are many ways in which one may take something without committing the crime of stealing, or kill someone without committing the crime of murder. Briefly put, the act itself may not be wrong (as in self-defense), the person may not know it was wrong (as in accidentally attacking a friend whom you think is an intruder about to hurt you), or the person may not understand what he or she is doing at all (as in a small child who doesn't know that a loaded gun is dangerous, or a demented or floridly psychotic person who literally doesn't realize what he or she is doing).

The legal requirements for being found not responsible (or not guilty) by reason of insanity vary slightly among jurisdictions, but always include the above concepts. Some states also consider whether or not the defendant was able to stop himself or herself from acting. In some states, the defense must prove the "insanity"; in others, the prosecution must prove "sanity."

Patients Involved with the Criminal Justice System

When treating patients who are awaiting trial or sentencing, one should be aware of the possibilities that symptoms will be exaggerated or malingered, that treatment will be used as a way to avoid something less palatable, and/or that the defendant will try to use the therapist in some future defense strategy. On the other hand, mental illness is over-represented among defendants and detainees, and the arrest and detention process itself can be quite stressful. Mental health services are often needed. The question of clinician *agency*[2] is very important in such settings (see below).

Patients in the Correctional System

Working with patients in prisons and jails who have already been found guilty (or, for children and adolescents, been "adjudicated") can be useful and rewarding. One should be aware of the limitations of correctional psychotherapy, and of the special countertransference

[2] Note that the word "agency," as used in this text, may have either of two quite different meanings. One connotes a government organization; the other, as here, connotes a clinician's role as an "agent" of some person or organization. "Dual agency" thus describes one's duty or responsibility to two different entities (one of which is usually a patient).

opportunities that exist, balancing the wish and obligation to help with the fact that the setting precludes truly unfettered therapy techniques. This is not a place for inexperienced clinicians, but experience can come quickly.

WHY CLINICIANS HAVE DUTIES THAT ORDINARY PEOPLE DON'T HAVE

An ordinary person walking down a street who sees a child drowning in a swimming pool and doesn't jump in to save him probably is not legally liable for his death. If you hear breaking glass and screams coming from your neighbor's house, you don't have to wrestle the intruder to the ground (although you may have some obligation to do *something,* such as call the police, to avoid being charged with a misdemeanor called "misprision of a felony").

So where do therapists get these "duties" everyone talks about? One source is your "special relationship" with patients and some other persons. Another is your special training, which, in part, is a foundation of that relationship. You may also incur duties by accepting a license to practice your profession, by being "on call" for someone else's practice, or by being an employee of or contractor for a health-care organization. While many lawsuits are dismissed because the plaintiff fails to prove a therapist–patient relationship (and thus the therapist is not held responsible for some damage that occurred because there wasn't a special relationship), professional responsibility may arise without one's ever seeing the patient (e.g., if the therapist covering a vacationing colleague's practice fails to be available for emergencies as agreed).

The "special relationship" is usually the key. Patients have a reasonable (and generally legally defined) expectation that a person who offers a professional service and/or agrees to perform professional services will perform the services within the applicable standard of care. That is, verifying your credentials and the quality of your care is not the patient's responsibility (no *caveat emptor* or "buyer beware" here); the patient has a right to expect proper qualifications and to receive the same care that any reasonable therapist in a similar situation would provide for similar patients. *A great many duties and responsibilities grow from the therapist–patient relationship.*[3]

Your license or other permission to practice also comes with certain duties and responsibilities. The license is a privilege, not a right, and the state exacts a *quid pro quo* for the privilege (e.g., the fee, the right to restrict licensees to those with certain qualifications, the right to evaluate your professional behavior, and the right to act as necessary to protect the public from dangers related to your practice).

A therapist–patient relationship creates a fiduciary duty. A fiduciary duty is one in which the fiduciary (that's you) has a strong legal obligation to act only in the best interests of (in this case) the patient.[4] This is a very important aspect of the clinician's work with the patient, and adds legal clout to the ethical guidelines discussed below. The concept of fiduciary duty also affects one's ability to assume other roles while (or even after) treating the patient. *In general, all of your other roles that may affect the patient (such as, but not limited to, managed care employee or contractor, agency employee, or expert witness) are subordinate to your fiduciary duty.*

Where does this leave clinicians who see patients for managed-care organizations, state agencies, correctional institutions, hospitals, and other employers or contractees that try to limit both the quantity and type of treatment offered? Let's say it again: You must place the patient's welfare above any of them, even if doing so is detrimental to your own interests. In particular, you must *at least* disclose to the patient any dual responsibilities or significant conflicts of interest that might affect him or her, including (but, as usual, not limited to):

- Patient interests *versus* the duty to be honest with an insurance payer
- Patient interests *versus* managed care or government agency rules
- Inmate-patient interests *versus* duty to the prison/employer
- Patient interests *versus* duty to be honest and objective in legal reports or testimony

[3] The relationship, and the duties and responsibilities that grow from it, are the same whether you call your patients "clients," "consumers," or something else.
[4] And, once again, you can't avoid your fiduciary and other duties and responsibilities by calling "patients" something else.

Many *evaluative* relationships—let's call the person an evaluee rather than a patient or client—do not create a fiduciary or clinician–patient relationship. Nevertheless, clinicians who evaluate people (not their own patients) for such purposes as employment, civil commitment, competency, criminal responsibility, sentencing, or child custody have a duty to disclose their agency—who they work for—and the purpose and possible consequences of the assessment.

Remember, the duties just described arise quickly, usually as soon as you begin seeing the patient or evaluee (sometimes even before; see page 22). Do not assume that you have no conflict of interest or dual agency just because you are an "independent contractor" rather than an employee. The fiduciary, agency, and/or ethical conflict is often independent of employee status.

See Chapter 3 for additional discussion.

LAW VERSUS STANDARD/DUTY VERSUS ETHICS

Civil duties, such as those just described, are not criminal matters. You can't go to jail (in the United States) for malpractice or other negligence. Criminal matters require, among other things, an *intent* to break the law (e.g., to harm someone). Nevertheless, your duty to meet the standard of care is recognized in every state and federal jurisdiction, and if someone is injured as a result of your breach of duty, you may be liable.

The standard of care that you must meet is not always clearly defined, nor is it usually defined in statutes themselves. Rather, state and federal statutes simply refer to your duty to meet the standard. They generally include a generic discussion of what "standard" should mean (such as "that care routinely offered by a reasonable physician in the course of managing a similar clinical situation"), but rarely offer specific examples.

Nevertheless, there is a standard. It is defined by several things, including the routine practice of other professionals, articles and studies in the legitimate clinical literature (as contrasted with anecdotal reports or nonscientific publications), and testimony from people the court has accepted as experts in that particular area of practice.

Ethical guidelines or canons are not matters of law, although they may be considered by the judge or jury (trier of fact) as evidence of practice within, or outside of, the standard, and they are often relevant to the legal concept of "fiduciary duty"(see above). "Official" professional ethics are promulgated by professional organizations, but have no standing outside the organization unless or until a licensing board or court decides to use them. If you're not a member of the American Psychological Association or the American Psychiatric Association, for example, the organization's internal rules simply don't apply to you (that's why I encourage patients to consider organization membership when they choose a therapist), although they may be considered by a court to suggest, or mirror, accepted practice.

Of course, being censured by a professional organization may trigger other negative events, such as license review or (for physicians) a listing in the National Practitioner Data Bank.

Negligence and Malpractice

Malpractice, which is a form of tort involving negligence, does not imply intentional harm. Under some circumstances, the negligence—and the potential for large monetary judgments—is greater than that for "ordinary negligence" (which is bad enough). If, for example, you are found "grossly negligent" or to have acted with "reckless disregard" for the consequences to the patient, it's a lot worse (but you still can't go to jail).

In order for a plaintiff to prove malpractice, he or she must convince the trier of fact, by a preponderance of the evidence (see above), that *all* of the following four conditions exist.

- A *duty* to the patient (see above)
- *Breach* or dereliction of that duty
- *Damage* to the patient (as a practical matter, the damage must be substantial)
- A direct relationship between the breach of duty and the damage (*"causation"*)

"Discharging" one's duty refers to carrying out the *legal* (but not necessarily the ethical or physically protective) requirements of a particular situation. If you have discharged some duty to warn or protect, for example, you have fulfilled it in the eyes of the law. This is not quite the same as saying you have "done all you can," or have met clinical or ethical guidelines.

There are a lot of other reasons—called "causes of action"—in addition to malpractice that one may sue. Many sexual boundary violation suits are not litigated as malpractice, for example. Hospitals and clinics that fail to keep their promises of care may be sued for the acts of their employees *(respondeat superior)* or for inadequate supervision, inadequate monitoring or communication, negligent appointment or credentialing, breach of contract (e.g., when conditions covered by an insurance contract are denied), and other things.

CONSENT

You can't do just anything you wish to a patient, even if it is therapeutic and in good faith. Every reader undoubtedly is aware of the general concept of "informed consent," but we need to delve more deeply into the subject.

First, consent does not always require an actual expression by the patient (or guardian[5]). The most common form of consent is "implied," that is, the patient passively allows the procedure or activity. This is the case for most psychotherapy patients, simple prescriptions, evaluations, and the like.

When consent is "expressed" (e.g., orally or in writing), oral consent is as valid as written consent, *provided the elements of valid consent are present* (see below). The problem, of course, is proving at some later time that the patient agreed. For most assessment and therapeutic activities (e.g., simple behavioral treatments and most psychotropic

[5] Unless otherwise noted, all references to consent generally apply also to legally substituted consent, such as that by a parent, guardian, or court.

medications), a simple chart notation by the clinician, before the treatment or other activity commences, that the patient has provided a valid consent is sufficient. Consent for procedures with significant risk (and some controversial ones with less risk) should be more carefully documented (e.g., with a formal procedure and written form).

Consent can be revoked at any time by a competent patient. If the sudden stopping of a treatment or procedure would endanger the patient, the clinician must use reasonable judgment in deciding how or whether to cease. If not revoked, a consent is generally valid until the treatment or procedure is over. For extended procedures (such as long-term psychotherapy or other chronic treatment), the clinician may wish to review the consent periodically to be certain that the patient understands and agrees. Some states may require such additional review and re-consent for specific procedures. If a procedure or treatment is substantially postponed after consent, an additional consent is advisable.

Specificity of Consent

Expressed consent may be valid only for specific procedures (e.g., extraction of the left lower incisor); however, most consents for psychotherapeutic interventions need only address the general form of treatment, expected benefits, and reasonably expected adverse effects (if any). Reviewing a detailed treatment plan with the patient is generally unnecessary unless the therapy carries unusual risk or controversy.

Side effects or adverse effects that are both rare and benign need not be exhaustively listed. There is a balance to be found between significance and likelihood. In medicine, for example, the risk of disability after a simple venipuncture (drawing blood) is so low that no warning is required (unless perhaps the patient is known to have a bleeding disorder). On the other hand, it may be necessary in some settings to discuss the very low risk of tardive dyskinesia with some acute neuroleptic treatments, and chronic use of these medications requires fairly complete disclosure.

Under special circumstances, it is permissible to keep information about adverse effects from a patient, for example, when a doctor believes a treatment is very important and the risk–benefit ratio is very favorable, but the patient would be so frightened by the discussion that he or she would not be able to judge the potential benefit rationally. Although this situation is not uncommon in severely and chronically mentally ill patients (for example, those who require antidepressants, electroconvulsive therapy [ECT], or antipsychotic drugs to alleviate morbid depression or psychosis), nonmedical psychotherapists should only rarely consider depriving the patient of information about adverse effects.

One of the currently "hot" areas in consent-related malpractice litigation is consent for intensive treatment of dissociative identity disorder (and some other conditions) in which a few therapists attempt to elicit (but often create) so-called repressed memories. As most readers know, memory is fragile and easily changed. When difficulties arise, many patients (or their families) allege that they were not warned of potentially severe problems associated with deep hypnosis or other "anamnestic" therapies.

Consent to release patient information is discussed in Chapter 9 on confidentiality and privilege. Copies of consent forms are provided in Appendix B. While not offered as legally complete, they are free of copyright restriction and may be copied (but not sold).

STATE—AND FEDERAL—LAWS GOVERNING PRACTICE

Most laws governing or influencing clinical and therapy practice are state laws, and, although broadly similar, vary from state to state, change over time, and cannot be adequately addressed in detail here. Although this book covers legal and forensic concepts relevant to clinical practice, it is not possible to keep up with every nuance of state and federal statute and case law.

It is important that the therapist be aware of the law, and there are many ways to stay informed. State and national clinical organizations can usually provide detailed information upon request (and often can influence legislation as well). Most therapists are already generally aware of applicable rules or laws about professional licensing and practice limitations, use of professional titles, reporting (abuse, clinician impairment, certain boundary violations, etc.), consent, and the like. Many are less knowledgeable about laws related to billing and charging (e.g., HCFA and state billing regulations, billing for teaching or supervision, or unlawful collection practices). Most therapists are uncertain about how to react to unexpected legal involvement, such as receiving a subpoena or summons or being sued. Many of these topics are discussed in later chapters.

PATIENTS' RIGHTS

Patients' rights are the foundation for much of the rest of this book. The "rights" do not have equal weight, however, and there is considerable misunderstanding about their relative strength and importance. Patients' Constitutional rights are generally based in the Bill of Rights, and include proscriptions against incarceration (e.g., civil commitment, involuntary seclusion) without due process, protection from abuse, and the like.[6]

Additional rights may be created by state constitutions, federal or state statute, or administrative rules with the force of law; however, these should not be confused with *Constitutional* rights. The U.S. Supreme Court, for example, has not interpreted the Constitution as providing any right to privacy or right to treatment, a fact often misunderstood by both professionals and laypersons.[7] "Right to treatment" is a *state* requirement in some states, but in many it is simply a commonly held philosophy.

[6] It's not a bad idea to review the Bill of Rights at some point, particularly if you practice in a hospital or correctional setting.

[7] As already mentioned, committed patients are Constitutionally entitled to "something more" (the U.S. Supreme Court's words) in return for their loss of liberty. The "something" has been interpreted in federal court as due process (not being committed without proper reason and procedure), adequate care (but not necessarily "treatment"), and protection from harm. Thus federal class-action lawsuits, which are commonly filed by the American Civil Liberties Union (ACLU) or U.S. Department of Justice against state mental health systems, are not technically about "right to treatment," but are about facility housing conditions, protection from abuse, and the like. Since such suits are usually settled out of court, the words "right to treatment" may appear in informal comments or news articles.

It is common to see a "Patients' Bill of Rights" posted in hospitals or published by a professional or advocacy organization. Unless such a document has been made part of a government administrative rule or agency policy, it too represents a philosophy or goal, not legal rights. Under some circumstances, however, it may be construed as a "standard" for purposes of creating a "duty" for clinicians or hospitals (see Chapter 3 on standards and policy).

· 3

ADHERING TO CLINICAL STANDARDS OF CARE

IN THE LAST chapter, we saw that fiduciary duties, other duties, and the therapist–patient relationship generate important responsibilities to patients and evaluees. Much of this chapter discusses these concepts under various practice conditions, usually concluding that those conditions do not always materially affect the way in which the civil law looks at standard of care. That is, the standard by which you are expected to practice your clinical profession is largely separate from your practice location or your source of payment. There are some nuances, however, that affect the clinician's risk of professional censure or lawsuit.

The standard of care begins with the establishment of a "duty of care." We will discuss many topics related to starting, stopping, or changing that duty, but it is wise to remember that it is easy to establish; a simple telephone conversation or the making of an appointment is often enough. Take telephone calls, brief crisis visits, referral conversations with colleagues, and the like seriously, not only from a clinical standpoint, but with regard to generation of a duty.

STANDARDS VERSUS FINANCIAL LIMITATIONS

Neither the law nor professional ethics requires therapists to work without compensation. With a few exceptions, private practitioners are generally free to decline patients who cannot pay or to terminate treatment of those who stop paying.

Initial Acceptance of the Patient

The simplest situation is that of declining the patient before any therapist–patient relationship has been formed. Unless you advertise otherwise (see below), you may legally and ethically verify the person's (note that I didn't say "patient's" at this point) ability to pay, and accept or decline work with him or her on that basis. This is best accomplished *before* forming any clinical relationship, and the therapist should make it clear that preliminary administrative activities, such as financial screening, do not create such a relationship (which may or may not be absolutely true; see below).

Clinicians sometimes offer an initial "low-cost, no obligation" *clinical* evaluation to determine whether or not a person will be accepted or is appropriate for care. Such visits may establish a therapeutic relationship even when one is not intended (and even if the person signs an understanding that he or she has not yet been accepted for care). For example, if you find the person to be in need of acute treatment (e.g., for psychosis, suicidal thoughts, acute deterioration), you may well be obligated either to provide adequate care or to see that it is available, regardless of whether or not you are paid. In an emergency, the duty increases still further. One should also remember that the duty exists whether or not you *recognize* the clinical problem, provided a reasonable mental health professional in your field *or in a field you are assuming* (see below) would have been able to recognize it. (Remember, the law is not only interested in what you knew and did, but also in what you *should* have known and *should* have done.)

Therapists who work for public agencies, managed-care organizations (MCOs), or other health-care (or mental-health-care) organizations often have little financial reason to decline patients. When the therapist has some responsibility for financial screening for the larger organization (e.g., by verifying the person's insurance), the general rules are the same as those just discussed. Being an agent of someone else does not change the rules to allow you to decline a duty of care on the other's behalf.

For therapists who work in public agencies and MCOs, the person may be your "patient" before you ever see him or her. The contract or relationship the patient has with the agency/MCO may have guaranteed such a relationship, and your role with the organization may obligate you to provide or obtain care.

Precertification or prospective utilization review of treatment or procedures does not determine, or generally affect, the standard of care. Although clinician-reviewers are sometimes considered to have a professional relationship with the patient, your own duty is not diminished by their decision. To repeat: The decision of a utilization or precertification reviewer, while sometimes couched in clinical terms (e.g., "not medically necessary" or "elective"), *does not affect your duty to provide or obtain care that you believe is necessary, as long as a clinician–patient relationship has been established.* There may be ways to discharge your duty other than treating the patient yourself, such as vigorously appealing the reviewer's decision or trying to obtain care elsewhere, but you must not "abandon" a patient who is entitled to your care. It is very wise to document such activities carefully.

When one procedure or kind of treatment is approved but another is not, the clinician has an obligation to discuss this with the patient and disclose the risks and benefits of both, limitations of the patient's insurance or health-care plan, alternatives available outside the current clinic or MCO, and any conflict of interest that might adversely affect the patient's care. These discussions should be documented as well.[8]

Diagnosing to fit reimbursement requirements is usually unethical and often illegal. If the diagnosis is purposely inaccurate, you have probably committed a crime. Furthermore, you have upset the actuarial and statistical surveys with which we estimate the incidence and prevalence of mental disorders. Don't insist that you were just trying to help the patient qualify for care; it's fraud.

---

[8] Clinicians' employment or MCO contracts should not contain prohibitions against such disclosures. When they do, the law generally places the patient's interest (remember "fiduciary") above your business obligation, if any, to the organization. As a practical matter, given recent publicity about the patient's "right to know," MCOs rarely enforce such contract provisions when good patient care is at issue.

Padding the diagnosis can backfire in other ways as well. Assume, for example, that you believe a patient has dysthymia, but you code something like "major depressive disorder" so that the insurance company will pay or the patient can be admitted to a hospital. Now assume that your treatment itself is aimed at the real (unwritten) diagnosis (dysthymia), while you write chart notes about vegetative signs and psychomotor retardation (to support your insurance diagnosis and mollify the utilization reviewers). Now assume that the patient commits suicide. Instead of having an arguable defense to a tragic outcome (i.e., that the patient did not show reasonably recognizable signs of major depression), you have a chart full of references to major depressive "red flags" and your treatment is devoid of careful monitoring for suicide risk, frequent follow-up, referral for adequate trials of antidepressants or consideration of ECT, and/or other indications that you took the risk seriously. I recently reviewed such a case, for a plaintiff's attorney.

Denying or Terminating Care for Financial Reasons

Once the patient is "yours," financial matters are a legitimate reason to limit or terminate care, provided (1) it is safe to do so and (2) the patient is not "abandoned." One should document the lack of need for acute care and the alternatives provided, and give the patient a reasonable time in which to find other care. Patients in intensive psychotherapy should be offered several sessions for transition or termination.

Abandonment must be avoided even when the current treatment need is not acute. It may not be enough to offer the names of several other therapists, particularly if one is not certain that the patient will be accepted by any of them. Similarly, recommending the local public mental health center may be inadequate because of waiting lists or entry requirements. It is best to continue to see the patient for some time while he or she searches for an alternative, with the clear understanding that unless there really is no alternative and the need is significant, your care will terminate on some specific date in the future.

A young adult patient with severe diabetes but no emergency need for care was difficult for her physician to "manage." She had a self-destructive lifestyle and regularly failed to follow the recommended treatment protocol. Her care was funded by Medicaid, which did not cover her many missed appointments and the extra time required of the doctor and his staff. After warning her several times to take her insulin, monitor her blood sugar, watch her diet, and follow his other instructions, the doctor finally told her (in person) that he could not see her anymore. A reasonable date was set for the termination of care and he gave her the names of three other qualified physicians. She didn't visit any of them, and called him several weeks later requesting an appointment. He politely refused, saying that she was no longer his patient, but provided more referral doctors' names. He did not contact any of the physicians himself, nor did he send them her records (although he would have provided her records and talked with any physician who called).

Several months later, the patient, apparently largely as a result of not following medical advice, required surgery for a lower-leg amputation (an occasional complication of severe, uncontrolled diabetes). In the interim, she had consulted several of the doctors the earlier physician had suggested, but each had declined to see her. Some refused because she was known not to cooperate with needed care; others may have balked because she was receiving Medicaid.

The patient sued the first doctor and won a substantial judgment for abandonment. The other physicians either were not sued or were not found liable (apparently because they had no treatment relationship with her).

STANDARDS VERSUS INSTRUCTIONS FROM EMPLOYERS OR CONTRACTORS

Employer or contractor instructions, even if codified in clinical protocols, may or may not meet or create a standard of care. The clinical standard is not built upon what some agency or MCO, for example, says should be done. Rather, the clinician must compare the protocol or instruction with legitimate reflections of the standard (such as current textbooks, professional studies and articles in peer-reviewed journals, or widespread practice outside the organization—no fair using the organization itself to define the standard). Organization policies that exceed the applicable clinical standard are discussed below.

Standards Versus Patient Requests or Social Pressure

Patient Requests

In spite of the fact that almost all counseling or psychotherapy is by patient request, and often at his or her own expense, your patient doesn't set the standard of care. He or she comes to you for competent (diagnosis and) treatment, not for an echo of his or her lay intuition (which is, in any event, likely to be colored by defensive wishes and fears). In fact, it is your duty to know what he or she needs, insofar as it is reasonable and within the standard to determine. A medical patient may voluntarily visit a doctor with a request that some pain be alleviated, but the doctor is the one who is *responsible* for the final diagnosis (even when the patient is right). The patient must agree to your therapy or other care, but should not dictate the technical process.

Experienced therapists know that unusual patient demands often connote, or portend, serious problems in the treatment relationship. If he or she demands a particular kind of treatment or some other consideration, you are the one who must determine whether or not it is the best approach (and what psychodynamic meaning the request may have), and then act accordingly. You are expected to recognize requests that are likely to interfere with the treatment (such as repeated requests for extra time at the end of therapy hours) and deal with them in a therapeutically appropriate way. Never accede to demands for unreasonable, unnecessary, or unethical care.

I'm not trying to be overly cold or conservative, but merely am pointing out that it is your duty to meet the standard, not the patient's, and the patient's requests or demands do not define the standard by which you may be judged.

Influence by social pressure may be seen more often in psychiatry than in the other mental health professions. Patients hear of the latest antidepressant and won't take No for an answer, or a psychiatrist may fail to recognize or explore a need for ECT because social controversy has made it difficult to obtain. As above, lay society is not the arbiter of the standard of care. If the medical literature suggests that ECT is indicated for a particular condition, the psychiatrist has a duty to consider it.

Other psychotherapists and counselors may be tempted to follow current styles and techniques (e.g., hypnosis for smoking cessation, "past-lives" therapy, or searching intently for sexual abuse in borderline patients' childhoods). To meet the standard, one should be convinced of the clinical value of the issue or technique, be properly trained and experienced, choose patients appropriately, and weigh—with the patient—the risks and benefits of proceeding. Good intentions are not enough.

PRACTICING OUTSIDE OR BEYOND YOUR PRIMARY QUALIFICATIONS

Practicing beyond one's training or specialty is a common way to practice outside the standard of care. *The standard is not defined by your background, but by the reasonable practitioners of whatever it is that you do.* That is, if a generically trained counselor practices cognitive-behavioral therapy (CBT) without specific CBT training and supervised experience, he or she is likely to be held to a cognitive-behavioral therapist's standard, not to that of a generic counselor dabbling in the technique. Similarly, a psychiatrist who administers and interprets psychological tests is held to the standard of a clinical psychologist, not to that of a psychiatrist dabbling in psychometrics. A therapist who accepts a patient with, say, depression has a duty to meet the mental health specialist's standard of care with respect to both treatment and recognition of complications (such as suicide risk), to recognize his or her professional limitations, and to refer those parts of patient care that he or she is unable or unwilling to provide to a qualified colleague (see shared or co-therapy, Chapter 4, for comments about liability related to such referrals). Your duty to practice at a "specialist" level is increased further if you represent yourself as, for example, competent to perform CBT or psychological test interpretation (e.g., by accepting referrals for such services, or advertising them).

Some therapists do not diagnose mental disorders, but either treat patients whose diagnoses have been made by someone else or treat symptoms without formal diagnosis. Most insurance plans require a specific diagnosis, and states, payers, and employers vary as to whether or not they accept, or even allow, diagnosis by nondoctoral professionals. If you diagnose without supervision, then you often have a duty to meet the same standard as more highly trained clinicians (such as psychiatrists or doctoral clinical psychologists) *and* to recognize the point at which a diagnostic issue should reasonably be referred to a doctoral colleague. Psychologists (and other therapists who choose to perform the same level of diagnosis) must either be able to recognize the point at which their patients require medical evaluation (and refer them for it) *or* routinely obtain psychiatric screening for them.

"Psychiatric screening" does not always mean evaluation by a psychiatrist. Psychiatry is a medical specialty that legally and ethically may be practiced by any licensed medical doctor. As implied above, however, that doctor must diagnose and treat to the same standard as a fully trained and qualified psychiatrist (but not necessarily the best one in town) *or* recognize the point at which the patient requires more expertise and refer him or her for specialist care *or* not accept the patient in the first place.

Psychiatrists and child psychiatrists are fond of saying that a family practitioner plus a psychologist does not equal a psychiatrist, and a pediatrician plus a child psychologist doesn't equal a child psychiatrist. In the eyes of malpractice liability, however, you really are whatever you hold yourself out to be. (If you make an *illegal* representation, such as practicing without a license, your problem is criminal, not malpractice. One of the Catch-22s of malpractice liability is that if you're not a real clinician, you don't have the duties of one.)

The patient does not have to assess whether or not you are competent; he or she is entitled to rely on you, as the clinician/therapist, to recognize your professional limitations and refer when necessary. *Psychiatry, psychology, and psychotherapy are not informal, intuitive talents. They require specific training and experience, and the patient has a right to expect expertise on the part of the professional, his or her recognition of professional limitations, and/or, when advisable, referral elsewhere.*

STANDARD VERSUS POLICY OR GUIDELINE

Plaintiffs' attorneys are fond of searching a hospital's or other health-care organization's own policies, procedures, and guidelines for evidence that a particular episode or professional behavior was below the standard of care. At first glance, the person and/or organization would seem to have fallen below the standard if the internal policy has been violated; however, policy alone does not make the standard (see above). In addition, policies and guidelines are often intended to exceed the standard, not merely to meet it, and to encourage excellence, not mere adequacy (which is all the standard requires). The duty is not for "perfect," or even "excellent," care, but for adequate care within a context of that which is reasonable for similar, qualified caregivers.

STANDARDS AND ADVERTISING OR PROMISES

People take clinical professionals seriously. Advertising—subtle or blatant—must meet standards of honesty and ethics beyond those of the average automobile dealer or computer store. We are not allowed the leeway of advertising "puffery" (arguably harmless exaggeration of advertising claims, such as, "We've got the best used cars in town").

When health-care organizations, such as hospitals or MCOs, advertise care above the usual standard of "adequate" or "reasonable" clinicians, the public may have a right to hold them to their promises. This has become a new cause of legal action against, particularly, MCOs. Competition has created some marketing claims that are pretty hard to live up to. Sometimes the liability falls to the health-care organization, and sometimes to those who depend on it to keep their promises.

A very large employer told its workers that all of their health-care needs would be met by a new company health plan. It then contracted with a managed-care organization to provide their medical care. When the MCO failed to meet that obligation by denying certain care to some of the employees, the employer was found liable for not making sure that the promise was kept.

In another case, a large multispecialty clinic and health maintenance organization (HMO) promised top-quality care. When its primary care and mental health professionals failed to promptly and properly diagnose and treat a severely depressed patient, who then committed suicide, the court heard evidence that the HMO and the clinicians not only should be held to the ordinary professional standard of care, but should be held to an even higher standard or else admit that their claim of excellence was dishonest.

VARIATION IN DUTY RELATED TO TYPE OF PATIENT RELATIONSHIP

Different clinician–patient relationships create different levels of duty. Simple evaluative procedures (not clinical consultations or evaluations for your own later treatment of the patient) generally do not even create a clinician–patient relationship (although you may wish to make this clear in a written notice; see Appendix B). The primary duties are to notify the evaluee of the nature and purpose of the evaluation, to do a competent job, and to handle the data and reports as required. There may or may not be a duty to recognize clear signs of danger or deterioration, and then either to report or to manage them in some way.

"Clinical consultations," defined here as clinical evaluations referred to you in a patient-care context, but in which you do not accept the patient for additional care or treatment, create similar duties, but usually add emphasis on recognizing clinical relevance and notifying the referral source promptly and completely.

Patients seen while on-call or covering a colleague's practice have a clinician–patient relationship with you, but you may not be required to review the case exhaustively before acting. It is up to you, however, to satisfy yourself that you have sufficient information to allow you to decide on a proper course of action. The primary (sometimes "attending") clinician has some level of duty to notify you of special patient needs or concerns before leaving the patient to your temporary care.

Emergency/crisis settings may lessen the clinician's duty to search the patient's records, take an exhaustive history, and so on. On the other hand, clinicians who work in crisis settings are expected to be trained and experienced in recognizing and treating the kinds of problems that are likely to arise. Emergency, crisis, and disaster settings are among the few in which the pressures of crowding and triage are an acceptable defense for abbreviated evaluation or care. Ordinary clinic crowding or overscheduling does not create such a defense, in my opinion.

Consultations or therapeutic activity by telephone should be carried out very carefully. There is no real substitute for seeing the patient in person, although certain telephone evaluations (and even prescribing) may be within the standard of care. The keys to remaining within the standard often include such things as (1) having substantial reason to believe that the patient is giving you reliable information, (2) having substantial reason to believe that the patient does not currently require more personal attention, (3) already knowing the patient and his or her situation well, (4) asking at least the same questions you would in person (and perhaps more, to make up for the lack of face-to-face contact), (5) assuring yourself that you have the necessary information with which to make a clinical decision and that the patient is very likely to follow through with it, (6) offering the patient the opportunity to see you or another qualified person in person if he or she wishes, and/or (7) offering some form of "call me back if it doesn't work" or "go to the emergency room" backup plan.

THE LEAST RESTRICTIVE CLINICALLY APPROPRIATE ALTERNATIVE

There is a kind of myth about the concept of a patient's right to the "least restrictive alternative." It has crept into mental health policy, objectives, and even laws, as if it were always a good thing. It isn't. Under many circumstances, it can hurt patients and others, and create liability for clinicians. Modified as in the heading of this section, with "clinically appropriate" added, the phrase makes a bit more sense. Unfortunately, not all policy makers and legislatures have added those critical words. After all, it sounds so *good* to guarantee patients' rights without any modifications. Much of the material here applies to psychiatrists and other physicians who make admitting or inpatient decisions. Comments related to commitment procedures and some restrictive outpatient programs also apply to other professionals whose licenses allow them to participate.

There are several situations in which one should be very careful about deciding the least restrictive clinically appropriate alternative, and careful about the pitfalls one must recognize when trying to balance the important issues of appropriate treatment, patients' rights, and the rights of others (viz., allegations of negligent or premature release, or failure to commit). Most are discussed elsewhere in this book; avoiding liability requires consideration and documentation of your choices from among the reasonable alternatives.

Do not assume that all those issues—appropriate treatment, patient rights, and the rights of others—can be well accommodated in every case. There are times when the clinician must make a decision rapidly, in the heat of a difficult situation. Your proper consideration of reasonable alternatives when recommendations or decisions must be made is more important than whether or not you can achieve perfection in that accommodation.

I suggest that safety be the first concern, but one should remember that these are almost never linear, mutually exclusive decisions. Some dangers are more significant than others; some patient needs are more critical, and some patient rights are more worthy of scrutiny, especially in acute treatment settings. Please do not misunderstand the last statement. No reasonable clinician wishes to deprive people of their civil rights, but sometimes the elevation of patient-care goals (and even mere niceties) to the level of "rights" trivializes the really important ones. It should be obvious that a "right" to wear one's own shoes on a psychiatric unit rather than hospital slippers, for example, is relatively less important than the right of another patient or staff person not to be kicked with hobnail boots. Similarly, two consenting patients' "right" to caress each other or to have sex is less important than their (and other patients') right to a nonsexualized treatment environment.

Individual negligence lawsuits almost always arise in a context of severe damage, such as a tragedy that can be associated with the clinician's or facility's care. One is rarely criticized for being overly protective of the patient or others (although it does happen), or for extra effort in diagnosis and treatment. This means that some clinicians fearful of being sued or criticized may substitute "safe" practices for slightly less safe but more therapeutic ones, to the ultimate detriment of most of their patients. Do not be cavalier or foolhardy, but remember that from the patient's viewpoint, he or she has come (or been sent) to you for specialized help, not primarily for rights enforcement or containment.

$\blacksquare 4$

PROFESSIONAL RELATIONSHIPS

MUCH OF THE patient's care, and the professional's liability, is related to relationships among clinicians and between clinicians and relevant laypersons or organizations (e.g., employers). Every relationship carries a series of duties, and thus some vulnerability to liability.

INDEPENDENT CONTRACTOR[9]

The most common compensated relationship for most therapists, except for the clinician–patient relationship itself, is that of "independent contractor." That is, one agrees to provide independent clinical services under certain condition(s) specified by the contractee, for some kind of payment. In most such agreements, the clinician is expected to be fully licensed and qualified, and to work within applicable law and ethical guidelines while fulfilling the contract.

By contracting, the organization or person offering the contract (called "contractee" below) can limit or eliminate many, but not all, of

---

[9] As used here, "contract" refers merely to an agreement in which the clinician exchanges a professional service for something of value. It is usually written, but need not be.

the responsibilities of "employer" while retaining the contractor's professional services. Readers should compare the things discussed immediately below with the duties and responsibilities of employers and employees addressed in the next section.

Since the patient is not the contractee, as would be the case when the patient or the patient's insurance pays the bill, a conflict of interest is created whenever the contract's purpose differs from the purpose of the clinical relationship (for example, when signing an agreement with an MCO that limits resource use). The clinician's fiduciary duty to a *patient* (not simply an evaluee, see Chapter 1) takes priority over any contract that tends to limit care, although disclosure of dual agency or other conflict to a competent and consenting patient may modify that priority.

Thus telling the patient that the MCO (or other organization) won't authorize certain (or further) treatment does not remove any therapist duties, but the patient's agreement to participate under those conditions—so long as all relevant information is provided to him or her and no emergency exists—may modify one's responsibility to go beyond the agreement. Nevertheless, *the clinician is almost always in a better position than the patient to determine the most appropriate clinical alternative. The patient does not give up the right to adequate care merely by agreeing to accept less; indeed, that right generally remains the patient's regardless of any consent or agreement.*

These principles apply as well to other duties, such as those of confidentiality (Chapter 9) and protection (Chapters 10 and 11), although these may not reach a fiduciary level. Thus a therapist who sees prisoners or parolees may adhere to nonclinical rules regarding security, and one who sees law enforcement officers or airline employees may be reasonably expected to tell the employer of known danger to the public.

The contractee has a right to expect that the contractor professional is licensed and otherwise qualified, but the contractee has some duty to verify those qualifications and monitor the clinical work. Although the contract or agreement often specifies that the clinician must meet certain conditions, the contractee should not rely solely on the contractor's own assurances; some form of verification of important qualifications and performance is usual. This is routinely done by such measures as demanding proof of qualifications, checking references, recredentialing from time to time, and conducting peer and performance reviews.

Both contracting organizations and others with professional relationships with clinicians (such as hospitals offering professional staff privileges) have a duty to exercise "reasonable care" in appointing, privileging, monitoring, and evaluating clinicians (see "Employer or Employee," below).

What Is in the Contract?

Therapists and other professionals should enter clinical contracts with both knowledge and caution. It is impossible to discuss contract issues completely in this chapter; however, several principles may be highlighted.

First, be aware of those duties and responsibilities that you cannot change or subrogate merely by signing a contract. Next, be very certain about what is demanded in exchange for your compensation. Do not accept any contract that is not completely filled in, and be particularly wary of items that refer to materials that are not supplied for your review. References to an organization's (e.g., MCO's) policies, rules, and the like should provide the complete wording of those sources; otherwise you are agreeing to provisions you have never seen.

Do not accept any requirement to keep business ("proprietary") data confidential when such confidentiality might interfere with the best interests of a patient. In some states, it is illegal for an MCO to prohibit clinician disclosures to patients about limitations on care, treatment alternatives, or your own conflicts of interest (e.g., financial incentives). In any event, it is often unethical, and below the standard of care, to keep such information from a patient.

Many third-party contracts, including most with MCOs, require the clinician to indemnify the contractee against claims arising from his or her care. Sometimes this is subtle, such as by requiring that the clinician carry malpractice insurance and that it be exhausted before the contractee accepts any liability. Other agreements blatantly say that the work of the contractor professional is completely separate from the contractee. Whether or not such wording will stand the scrutiny of litigation, it exposes the clinician to far more trouble than necessary, and one agrees to it at his or her peril.

Whenever possible, contracts should be reviewed by one's own attorney and malpractice carrier. The malpractice carrier understands legal duty and standard of care, and can help you determine whether or not the contract exposes you to unusual liability or something that may not be covered by your policy.

Finally, it is foolish to sign a contract hurriedly, or just because it is "our routine agreement." The contract value goes beyond the dollar value of the agreement, to protecting one's assets and professional reputation.

EMPLOYER OR EMPLOYEE

Employers of clinicians incur a number of responsibilities. Health-care organizations add considerable potential liability when they employ clinicians rather than contracting with them or entering into noncontract voluntary arrangements (e.g., private hospital professional staff relationships).

A longstanding legal doctrine called *respondeat superior* makes an employer generally responsible for the acts of the employee. This means that when a negligent employee with little money or insurance causes damage to a patient or client, a plaintiff may be able to recover from his or her supervisor or organization. In many organizations, such as government agencies like community mental health centers, individual supervisors are relatively indemnified because the responsibility passes to the agency or the government itself. There are exceptions to *respondeat superior* for actions that are outside one's job parameters and some *discretionary* activities (i.e., those not completely under employer control, such as clinical supervision) in some jurisdictions.

Federal, state, and local governments often limit their vulnerability through laws designed to protect them from liability for good-faith acts or limit the maximum amount that can be recovered. Clinician-employees and supervisors should not take too much solace in these *relative* protections from lawsuit, however, since attorneys can often find some way to compensate injured plaintiffs, and find access to clinical employees' assets, when negligence and damage are clear.

Employers have a duty to exercise "reasonable care" (or some similar term in different jurisdictions) in hiring, privileging, monitoring, evaluating, censuring, and terminating employees, including clinicians. The patient has a right to rely on the organization to provide licensed, qualified professionals and to monitor them from time to time to make sure that they are doing a good job. It is not enough for the employer to claim that it "didn't know" about a problem clinician's background; the organization must take acceptable steps to discover problems, and sometimes to anticipate obvious future potential for negligence.

A hospital therapist was accused of abusing several patients, and both the therapist and the hospital were sued. Since the abusive acts were clearly outside his professional assignment, the hospital attempted to dissociate itself from any liability. The plaintiff's expert reviewed the therapist's personnel and credentialing files[10] and found that there was no reference from his last place of employment, and no explanation for a several-year period in which he listed no professional activities. Further research revealed that if the hospital or credentials committee had inquired, it would have discovered that the therapist had had significant problems, and had been unable to practice for some time because of a suspended license. This information, which is likely to have established liability for the hospital, was instrumental in encouraging the hospital to settle out of court for a great deal of money.

Employers have a duty to deal fairly with the professionals who work for them. For mental health professionals, censure or termination that affects one's reputation is far more damaging than, for example, merely losing one's job.

An employee who was also a graduate clinical trainee had an intimate relationship with a staff member at a field clinic (which was organizationally separate from his employer and training program). The woman involved was unmarried, and was not his employee, employer, supervisor, or supervisee. After several weeks, the staff person reported that he had harassed her. The evidence for

---

[10] Although the actions of hospital credentials committees are confidential in many respects, their files are often "discoverable" in lawsuits (particularly if their contents are germane to a hospital's or clinician's defense).

any harassment was quite vague. His employer terminated him within a few hours of the complaint, his trainee status was revoked, and the police were notified. All of this was baffling to the trainee, who readily admitted that they had a relationship and that it might have been poor judgment to become involved with a clinic employee, but denied doing anything nonconsensual.

The trainee appealed, and obtained legal counsel. An administrative law judge found that he had been terminated without "due process" and the employer offered to reinstate him while they reprocessed his termination using the appropriate administrative procedures. The trainee, through his lawyer, did not accept the settlement and, at this writing, is considering a lawsuit for wrongful termination and damage to his career, alleging that the employer overreacted to the possibility of a sexual harassment lawsuit and attempted to sacrifice him to decrease its exposure. (Note that wrongful termination actions tend to be much less expensive for defendants than are accusations of sexual harassment.)

A clinician or counselor who is (or represents) the employer must be cautious about developing conflicting relationships with employees. The old saying that the boss should be "friendly, but not your friend" contains a lot of wisdom for both employee and supervisor. Setting aside the merely uncomfortable situations of business or professional decisions being complicated by personal relationships, there are times when apparently benevolent acts are easily construed as legally inappropriate and damaging to the employee.

A prominent mental health professional in a large agency was showing increasingly poor performance and was in danger of termination. A senior manager, also a clinician, noted that the woman appeared to have symptoms of emotional impairment and quietly began to intervene with "informal" talks and occasional counseling. The manager believed that she was just trying to be helpful and that there was no therapist–patient relationship. When the employee-professional divulged bizarre thoughts and behavior, only some of which were obvious to others, the manager feared that patients—or the employee-therapist herself—might be in danger. She quietly contacted the agency director (who was not a professional, but was considering options to correct the performance problem) and the therapist's husband. The husband seemed grateful for the call, saying that he had been very worried and that the therapist had once agreed to a clinical evaluation but had "fooled the psychiatrist."

The therapist was eventually terminated and sued the clinician-manager for breach of privilege, misrepresenting her role, and slander. She alleged that a therapist–patient relationship had been created and that calling her husband and boss amounted to a breach of a clinician's obligation to maintain confidentiality. She also claimed that the manager had described her inaccurately, unfairly caused the agency director to doubt her performance, and damaged her marriage. Finally, the employee criticized the manager for assuming a dual role of "counselor" (whether informal or not) and management representative. It would have been far better not to offer even informal direct counseling, to suggest a referral outside the agency (even to an employee assistance program, or EAP), and, however painful, to watch from a distance as events ran their course.[11]

Employee-clinicians do not give up their fiduciary relationship with their patients. In spite of the doctrine of *respondeat superior* (above), professionals who are qualified and empowered to make independent decisions (i.e., have legal or professional discretion to act independently even though employed, such as doctors or therapists) generally retain at least some independent liability as well. It is difficult to sue military clinicians and some other government doctors and therapists, but one should not be completely reassured that his or her employer absorbs all of the potential liability for clinical acts. As a practical matter, an uninsured professional usually has few individual assets of interest to plaintiffs (as compared with employers or contracting organizations); however, a fat malpractice insurance policy quickly makes one a logical additional target for litigation.

When you employ nonprofessionals, such as secretaries, receptionists, or even cleaning people, you have a duty to search applicants' backgrounds for indications that they may harm your patients. You must also have and discuss, in at least a rudimentary way, your rules

---

[11] "Official" in-house employee counseling services are an exception, provided the boundaries of their services are clear, dual relationships are divulged, and limitations on confidentiality (such as disclosing danger to patients, public, or self) are understood. Most organizations prefer to refer elsewhere; some retain independent EAP contractors.

about such issues as confidentiality, train them appropriately, monitor employee behavior, and take suitable action if problems arise.

Even with rules in place, such things as the professional obligation to maintain patient privilege and privacy are your responsibility, both ethically and under the doctrine of *respondeat superior* (above). The same concerns apply when you are not the employer, but such people have access to your patients and their records (e.g., files left unlocked overnight). Even when you are not responsible for the training and monitoring, you should satisfy yourself that patients are protected as well as is reasonably feasible. Be especially cautious in rural or unsophisticated settings (see Chapter 6).

THERAPIST SUPERVISOR (NONEMPLOYER)

This section refers to "official" supervision—that related to training, clinical team oversight, new employee monitoring, or paid supervisory consultation. It does not refer to ordinary consultation or "co-therapy" (see below) in which there is no clear supervisory component.

When a supervisor has control of or direct influence on patient care, he or she assumes many of the same risks as accrue to a clinician–patient relationship. It is important for supervisor and supervisee (and any invested third parties, such as a training program or employer) to have a clear, perhaps written, understanding of supervisory parameters and expectations. In clinical team oversight, for example, the supervisor is often expected to see the patient, and perhaps to perform certain evaluations or treatments in person. At the other end of the spectrum, the standard for privately arranged psychotherapy supervision does not require personal interaction with the patient. The standard usually does not require supervisors of independently licensed professionals to be continuously available; however, there are circumstances—related to both the supervisory understanding and the patient's predicted needs—that mandate close monitoring and/or availability.

Case-limited supervision is at once more, and less, demanding than general or topic-centered supervision. When following the care of one patient, the supervisor is expected to keep up with his or her care in some detail, guiding both the regular clinical work and the management of problems that arise, and often monitoring the therapist's feelings and issues as well. This expectation may well reach the level of a "duty" to the patient and thus create potential liability. If one is supervising a general caseload, on the other hand, the overall responsibility is greater, but it is reasonable to assume that the supervisory involvement may focus on known problem situations rather than on following the details of everyday care.

Supervisory responsibility should not be taken lightly. It is flattering to be asked to supervise a colleague or trainee, but one should understand that one will then become a part of the patient's care (or the care of many patients, if the supervision is general rather than case oriented). Your relationship may *seem* to be solely with the therapist, but it is wise to act as if it is also with his or her patient(s). Supervisors should meet regularly with the therapist and make some effort to be sure that they obtain all the relevant patient information (e.g., by reviewing the patient chart, reading the supervisee's therapy notes, and/or listening to session audio- or videotapes). Sitting in on sessions is generally unnecessary, and audio or video recording, while suggesting that the supervisor is taking his or her role seriously, is not required by the standard of care. If recordings are made as part of the supervision or therapist-monitoring process, the supervisor probably has a duty to review at least parts of them. In my opinion, however, it is acceptable to rely on the therapist for much of the information (i.e., it is unnecessary, in terms of the standard of care, to listen to each session verbatim just because there is a tape of it).

The supervisor should discuss supervision rules and contingency plans for problems in advance, and the patient should be made generally (but not obsessively) aware that a highly trustworthy and qualified third person will have access to clinical information. No matter what the style of supervision (e.g., case-limited, general, topic-centered), the therapist must not hold back information from the supervisor, and should never promise a patient that some bit of information will be kept "just between us." Sharing information with one's supervisor is not a breach of privilege or confidentiality. The temptation to censor patient or therapist material for one's supervisor, no matter what the conscious reason, suggests countertransference or other problems that, conversely, *need* discussion.

"Topic-limited" supervision is a phrase I made up just for this book. It refers to supervision that is not merely *centered* on a particular topic, such as the therapist's cognitive-behavioral technique, but purports to be *limited to it*. Like a lot of things I make up, it may not really exist (in the world of duty and liability, at least). If you are asked to supervise (not just "consult, but to have some control over the clinical/therapeutic process) only one aspect of care, you should be aware that if the overall care is within your general area of expertise, a plaintiff's lawyer may allege that you also have a duty to recognize and deal with significant problems outside the narrow subspecialty area. For example, a family therapy supervisor who is expert in relationships and networks is likely to have a duty to recognize and deal properly with suicide potential or substantial potential for child abuse. Similarly, a clinical psychologist supervising the psychotherapy of a patient taking psychotropic medications should be able to recognize *obvious* side or adverse effects (and then recommend appropriate referral for medical assessment), but not subtle ones.

One is not required to recognize things far outside one's area of expertise, or to direct the treatment of them, as long as the primary therapist is aware of those limitations. It is wise to document a disclosure to the supervisee that, for example, "We are to limit our discussions to the supervisee's hypnotic induction technique (or "the use of negative behavioral reinforcers"). She understands that other aspects of the patient's evaluation and care will be supervised by Dr. Smith, and I do not expect to become aware of details of the overall treatment." Recognize, though, that you are expected to recognize and do what a well-trained and experienced supervisor in the same field would reasonably be expected to recognize and do.

Note the phrase "well-trained and experienced" in the last sentence. If you represent yourself as qualified to supervise, if you dabble in some special form of therapy and then supervise others in its use, or if you allow yourself to be assigned a supervisory or oversight role (e.g., by an MCO or training program), *then you will be held to the same standard as would be a well-trained and experienced therapist in that subspecialty*. Know your limits, be alert for signs that they are being approached, have ways of dealing with them in the patient's interest (e.g., by referral), stay out of situations in which you are not professionally comfortable, and *do not misrepresent your professional abilities to a patient or supervisee.*

CONSULTANT

Some of the best liability (and, more important, clinical) advice I've heard came in three words from Harvard psychiatrist Dr. Thomas Gutheil:

Never worry alone.

Like most Texans, I hate deferring to the Ivy League, but Tom deserves the credit for reducing great advice to a memorable *bon mot.* Memorize it.

From the treater's or evaluator's point of view, when important doubts about assessment or care arise, there are almost always ways to reduce them, and one of the best is to get advice from a peer or subspecialist. You do not need the patient's permission to do this. I cringe when I hear a psychiatrist or psychotherapist try to convince a jury that he or she couldn't ask for a second opinion about a patient's suicidal behavior because of "confidentiality." No state, so far as I know, limits clinical consultation intended in the patient's interest. (Notice that I did not say you could consult his employer or girlfriend without permission; we're referring to qualified clinicians.) Even if you are concerned about breach of confidentiality, (1) it may be possible to get a verbal consultation without revealing the patient's identity and (2) I would much rather help your lawyer defend your good-faith effort to obtain consultation than your alleged negligence after the patient is involved in some tragedy.

Of course, if either you or the consultant believes that the consultant should see the patient in person, the patient will have to agree in most cases (but not all; cf., civil commitment assessments, assessments for other involuntary care, emergencies, certain incompetent patients). The patient's agreement need not be formal (as in writing), but may merely be reflected in a positive response to a comment, such as, "Since we talked about (depression, medication, substance abuse) at our last visit,

I've asked a specialist, Dr. Jones, to be available to meet with us today; is it O.K. if she comes in?" *or* "While you're in the hospital, it seems important to get another professional view of your (depression, memory lapses, relationship with your wife). I'd like for a colleague with some special expertise to visit with you while you're in the hospital." Even if you don't wait for the patient's verbal expression of approval, his or her passive acceptance and later voluntarily talking with the consultant are generally sufficient to establish consent for the consultation.

An atmosphere of extortion or deceit decreases, but may not completely destroy, the validity of informal consent to consultation. Such things as threatening a patient with seclusion if he or she doesn't meet with the consultant may be viewed as patient abuse in some settings. Telling the patient (often an adolescent, depressed, or psychotic patient) that the consultant is there for some innocuous purpose when it is really for, for example, a commitment evaluation arguably destroys the value of the consent, is generally unethical, and often decreases clinical validity as well.

Both primary clinician and consultant should know that consultation is not a binding process. It may influence the primary clinician's care or recommendations to the patient, but it is not the same as "supervision." In general, consultation relationships are with the primary clinician, not the patient (but see the next paragraph), and the clinician is allowed to take or leave the consultant's advice. The standard of care generally requires that the primary clinician be competent to weigh that advice in the patient's interest; if it is unclear, the clinician should take reasonable steps to clarify it (e.g., by talking with the consultant or gathering knowledge or information from other sources). The consultant has a duty to be competent in his or her task, but this usually means being complete and expert, not making the final decision or following the patient.

The "relationship" statement above does not apply if the patient is referred for something like "consultation and follow-up" or "consultation and appropriate treatment." When the consultant and patient accept this kind of referral, a clinician–patient relationship is quickly formed, with all the attendant duties and responsibilities discussed in Chapter 2. Thus a consultant should not prescribe tests or treatment, or even give specific advice (which is a kind of "prescribing"), unless it is clear that this is his or her role, or there is some emergency. Doing so may establish a clinician–patient relationship. It is also unwise to suggest to the patient that the primary clinician will do some specific thing (e.g., start conjoint or psychoanalytic psychotherapy), since the clinician may or may not decide to do it. On the other hand, a consultant who recognizes, or should recognize, an emergency or other acute condition requiring specific attention to prevent damage to the patient or others probably has a duty to take some form of protective action. The action should be proportional to the patient's need, and may not necessarily involve direct clinical intervention (e.g., promptly notifying the primary clinician may be sufficient, provided one makes sure that he or she got, and understood, the message).

CO-TREATER (DIVIDED TREATMENT)

We discussed co-treatment briefly in Chapter 1. I'll say again that it is very easy for the concept of co-treatment to overlap with some duty to supervise, protect, or at least monitor the other clinician's care. In any event, co-treaters are responsible for knowing something about—and approving—the credentials, treatment style, and ethics of those with whom they share treatment or to whom they refer patients.

Coverage, Substitute Therapists

The same principles apply to colleagues with whom you share clinical coverage or "call." When you leave the patient, overnight or for a month's vacation, you have a duty to make competent coverage available for reasonably predictable problems (although not problems that are well outside your area of expertise, such as heart attacks or outbreaks of psoriasis). This is particularly important for patients who are being treated for acute disorders or are known to be unstable (as contrasted with highly functioning patients in stable psychodynamic work, for example), those whom you do not know well, those with a potential for suicidal or other destructive behavior, and the like. The rule is simple: Be sure you have adequate, competent coverage. The corollary is simple, too: *You have a duty to know, to a reasonable extent, when any clinician associated with your professional practice or on-call roster lacks the ability, experience, or character necessary to meet his or her obligations to your patient, and to avoid placing your patient in that person's care* (or potential care, in the case of on-call coverage). The duty *may* be discharged by relying on acceptable credentialing procedures, licensing boards or records, professional references, and/or your personal experience with the clinician.

PROFESSIONAL OR EMPLOYEE REFERENCES

Health-care employers, licensing or certification agencies, professional staff groups, and the like rely on professional references to determine clinicians' and employees' eligibility to care for (or simply have access to) patients. Persons who provide those references have a duty to avoid lying to or misleading the correspondent, by either commission or omission. Once one decides to give a reference, both specific questions and open-ended ones (such as, "Do you know of anything that might limit this clinician's ability to treat patients safely and competently?") must be answered completely and honestly.

We all want to help friends, and no one wants to be the one to keep a colleague from his or her work. In today's litigious environment, especially given the career implications of even one refused license or privilege, we even fear being sued for being honest. Nevertheless, *if you knowingly mislead an employer, clinic, licensing agency, or similar credentialing body about a clinician's suitability for practice, and the clinician is involved in some negligent (e.g., malpractice) or intentional (e.g., sex with patients) tragedy, you may be sued for being one of the factors that led to his or her being in the situation.*

Many employers have a firm personnel policy against providing detailed references for former employees or consultants. They believe they can limit their liability by providing the same simple reference for everyone, perhaps just listing the dates of employment and including a statement that the person left in good standing. This is not a situation in which Thumper's mother's advice is relevant, however. ("If you can't say somethin' nice, don't say nothin." —*Bambi.*) *In my opinion, such a policy should not apply to professional references; it is not fair to future patients, and does not meet the duty of a clinician to protect the interests of potential patients.* The clinician (and, arguably, the organization) who supplies a reference for another clinician whom he or she knows is likely to practice unsafely or incompetently should place the interests of future patients above the personnel policy. In fact, many state medical licensing boards require physicians to report colleagues whom they have reason to suspect are impaired or incompetent.

Of course, both adverse and positive comments must be based on personal knowledge or reliable evidence. Rumor and innuendo do not constitute "good faith" and, in addition to being unfair to the clinician, leave one open to charges of libel and slander. If you don't know, decline to provide a reference.

· 5

RELATIONSHIPS WITH PATIENTS AND FAMILIES

ACCEPTING OR DECLINING PATIENTS

A<small>LMOST ALL VULNERABILITY</small> to professional negligence allegations arises from the special relationship between doctor/therapist and patient. Although uncommon, there are times when it is prudent not to accept a patient and the accompanying responsibility. There are also times when you simply don't wish to accept a patient.

The clinician generally has a right to decline a patient, for whatever reason. There are exceptions, such as when one has responsibility for crisis or emergency services (in which the emergency patient has a right to expect competent services from the clinician on duty and cannot be "dumped" from the care setting if proper care would be threatened), or perhaps (but not always) when working with assigned patients is part of one's employment or contract. For the most part, though, the decision is yours. Unless you work for an organization to which the patient has some right to access, such as a public clinic, it is ethical to decline a nonemergency patient because you believe that he or she cannot (or will not) pay for your services, or might disrupt your practice, or simply because you don't want to see that patient.

There are times when you *should* decline a new patient. Remember, by accepting the patient, you are representing to him or her that you will meet the standard of care. If you know, or reasonably should know, that you can't meet that standard, it is improper to accept the patient. An employee of a clinic or MCO may not be able to pick and choose patients on the basis of preference alone, but if you believe you cannot competently and safely work with the patient, you should not accept the assignment.

Sometimes having clinical skills is not sufficient reason to accept a patient. If, for example, you know that you are easily seduced by hysteroid or borderline patients, have trouble controlling your anger at substance abusers, or have deep personal feelings about child abusers, supervision or consultation alone may not be the answer. Consider a patient load that fits your style and person (and even your psyche), as well as your skills.

If one wishes to avoid a clinician–patient relationship, *one must not delay declining it, and must be careful not to create a special relationship after declining.* It is difficult, legally speaking, to set aside your professional status; even a friendly bit of advice may be construed as a professional act. As mentioned earlier, a professional relationship may occasionally be formed by something as simple as a telephone conversation or scheduling an appointment.

BILLING

Billing is rarely an issue of professional standard, but it can be associated with feelings in patients that lead to projection, dissatisfaction, feelings of entitlement, or the belief that the therapist himself or herself thinks that he or she did something wrong. Fraudulent billing may be a criminal matter (e.g., billing for services not actually rendered, for diagnoses known to be inappropriate, or, in some cases, for services rendered in your name without your being present).

Billing most affects the clinician–patient relationship when the billing process is unusual. Problems are less likely when it is matter-of-fact and consistent among patients. Questions about charges or billing should be handled the same way. Your rules (or those of the agency or organization for which you work) concerning charges, payment schedules and expectations, and what happens when payment gets behind, should all be discussed. It is a good idea to provide the rules in writing.

Experienced therapists know that these matters are best handled just as any other business arrangement, so that they either stay out of the way of the therapeutic relationship or transference issues regarding them are easily spotted.

"Special" billing arrangements make the patient "different" and are associated with an increased opportunity for misunderstanding (real, displaced, or projected) and, when countertransference rears its head, improper or substandard care (cf., treating VIP patients). Barter payment arrangements can be especially problematic. Money is a very consistent medium of exchange, and patients' reactions to it are reasonably predictable and understandable by the therapist (and judge or jury, if it comes to that). Trading clinical services for other items, such as goods or services, although not illegal or necessarily unethical, complicates treatment and increases the probability of boundary and transference–countertransference problems. The same comments apply to free or discounted care. *Note that the standard of care is the same whether you charge a little or a lot, barter, discount or delay the fee, see the patient "pro bono," bill directly or through an MCO or insurance company, or work for an organization that pays you a salary.*

Overdue Accounts

First, reread the last sentence of the paragraph above.

Overdue accounts should be dealt with in a consistent, matter-of-fact way (but you need not emulate Ebenezer Scrooge). Your collection practices should meet local and federal criteria. Referral to a collection agency requires some attention to confidentiality, but can usually be accomplished by following professional organization guidelines. After all, the patient is the one who owes the money; he or she is not generally allowed to tie your financial hands merely by citing privilege.

You may stop treating a patient for nonpayment (or any other reason, for the most part). Most readers will have done so several times by the time they get around to reading this book. The most important legal and ethical point here is your duty to avoid *abandoning* the patient and damaging him or her in the process.

You must give reasonable warning, not leave the patient without a way to continue current acute or emergency care, and provide some avenue through which he or she may seek other, needed care. (Note that these duties apply to a person who is already your patient, not to someone with whom you have no clinician–patient relationship; see above.) For some patients, the process can be accomplished by giving a couple of weeks' notice and supplying the names of two or three other therapists or agencies you believe may accept them. Patients who are acutely ill, unable to take responsibility for contacting a clinician themselves, in danger of suicide or other harm, or reasonably expected to deteriorate as a result of stopping your treatment should be carefully "handed off" to a competent colleague who is willing to accept responsibility for their care.

There is an old axiom in private psychotherapy that says that it is better to have the patient owe a bank, or even a relative, than the psychotherapist. I agree; not allowing the patient to go into debt to the therapist prevents many potential problems. Incidentally, being a "nice" therapist and allowing the bill to go unpaid for more than a short time probably doesn't decrease the probability of litigation. The money will become a larger and larger issue in the clinician–patient relationship. The patient will become "special" in some negative way (although he or she may think it's positive, that you are expressing fondness by not demanding payment). You may actually give a different, less expensive, or less frequent kind of treatment (perhaps thinking that differential treatment is justified by the financial issue). If the problem is acute or involves danger to the patient, it isn't justified. The patient may project guilt or shame related to nonpayment onto you and, for example, denigrate your services.

LITIGIOUS PATIENTS

Dealing with litigious patients was one of the most common concerns among respondents to our psychotherapist survey (although far behind "managed care"). If you know that a patient will place you at high risk for litigation, you probably don't have to accept him or her (see above). Litigious patients have problems too, but that doesn't mean you have to see them.

More commonly, a therapist realizes at some point in treatment that his or her patient is threatening, extorting, impossible to mollify, and/or so unreasonable in treatment expectations that the working relationship seriously deteriorates.

Practice well. Do and recommend what you think is clinically best for the patient. Reassure yourself and the patient with consultation. Document your care and communications extensively, including patient comments and behavior. If you are very concerned, consider recording your sessions (even though it may make the treatment less routine and more "special"). Tell the patient that you will be recording, and that recording is often routine in therapy. If he or she objects, consider ceasing treatment (with appropriate procedures to protect the patient and avoid abandonment).

Communication is arguably the most important key to avoiding litigation. Most of us assume that because we know a lot about communication, we must be good at it ourselves. For many mental health professionals, however, nothing could be farther from the truth. We often confuse stereotypic personal openness with good communication, and mistake feelings for honesty and the search for true understanding.

Personal openness doesn't prevent lawsuits, nor does being a nice person. People sue for two main reasons: they believe they've been wronged, or they're mean and dishonest. The belief that one has been wronged may arise in two ways: through real wrong or through perceived wrong. If you've done something wrong that substantially damaged the patient, you are vulnerable to allegations that it arose out of negligence or malicious intent, and being nice might affect what the patient does. In litigious patients, however, the feeling that one is wronged arises more from within the patient (or the patient's family) than from the therapist's behavior. Of course, if the patient is just mean and dishonest, it is pointless to waste your niceness trying to mollify him or her.

Do not act outside the margins of what you believe is safe and competent care. You have no duty to please or agree with the patient, but you must practice within the standard of care. It is improper, and may be malpractice or even illegal, to accede to a patient's request when you don't believe it is clinically appropriate.

Don't let your patient extort you. Resist the temptation to please the patient, or seemingly to make your life less complicated, by changing a diagnosis to fit a job or insurance need, certifying nonexistent disability, prescribing or recommending unnecessary medication, and so on. These acts are unethical at best and illegal at worst, and if you do it once, you have damaged the patient's trust, the therapeutic relationship, and your own self-image and career. You may think at first that the treatment relationship will be strengthened if you accede to such a request (or demand). You may even rationalize your behavior with such logic as, "If I don't diagnose major depression, the insurance company won't pay and the patient won't be able to continue needed therapy," or "He may be able to work, but if I say he's disabled, he'll be motivated to continue therapy."

Bull pucky. It's dishonest, and you're telling the patient that you think it's fine for both of you to become criminals for the price of a few sessions or a disability check. The patient may be *more* likely to sue you after that kind of behavior, since you are now a better target for his or her rationalization, externalization, displacement, and projection (and you may have a hard time convincing a jury that you are honorable if the record shows you acted improperly at some prior time).

Therapists who feel extorted by patients are rarely at their best, probably make more mistakes, and have trouble enjoying life. If you feel yourself moving into a troublesome position, get clinical or legal consultation (remember, "never worry alone"). Professional organization (e.g., APA) legal plans have considerable experience in such matters, and such organizations are good resources for ethics queries. You need not notify the patient of the consultation, but you may wish to do so. Not telling him or her may create a "secret" that is unconsciously conveyed to the patient, who then has all the more reason to project or displace; and if the patient finds out later, you may be accused of going behind his or her back.

Finally, while it may be helpful to discuss your concerns about lawsuits with the patient or family, do not waste time and energy exacting a promise that you won't be sued. It is improper to make clinical care contingent on such a promise. Further, since a person cannot easily give away a civil right, the promise is almost certainly not enforceable.

PROFESSIONAL STYLE AND AVOIDING LAWSUITS

After all this defensive-sounding discussion, let's return to some obvious, preventive steps. There are several personal and psychodynamic issues that increase litigiousness. Watching for and dealing with such things as personal and family loss; chronic mental or physical illness; antisocial, "borderline," and other character traits; deep feelings of entitlement; substance abuse; past therapy difficulties; or past litigation brings the issues to the surface at least, and may prevent them from getting out of control.

Allegations related to lack of consent for a procedure or treatment can often be traced to lack of patient or family participation in decision making. When you get a formal consent, be sure it isn't merely a *pro forma* experience. In managed-care or other settings that are rigid in their therapy choices, try to help the patient understand and feel that he or she is participating in the process.

Do not be defensive about your work, but don't be arrogant, either. If there has been a tragedy or bad treatment outcome, offer sympathy, but do not automatically assume blame. Your malpractice carrier is a good source of advice in specific situations.

COVERAGE AFTER HOURS AND DURING VACATIONS, AND CALLS AT HOME

You have a duty to provide competent coverage for emergency needs related to your clinician–patient relationship. Different patients and therapy styles suggest different levels of emergency availability, but almost all can be accommodated with an on-call roster, crisis line, or 24-hour emergency setting. You need not provide the crisis or emergency coverage yourself, but you must arrange for it and communicate the arrangement to your patients. For patients likely to have serious problems, critical patient information (e.g., suicidal or homicidal threats, important prescriptions) should be reasonably available for rapid communication to an emergency clinician.

The need for availability of information is often dealt with by communicating potential problems to the on-call person (e.g., having a brief conference at the end of the day to tell him or her about patients who might call and current patient problems). In organized clinics, critical records should be available through an emergency number, and the niceties of informed consent dispensed with when the request involves danger to life or limb. Mental health clinics that are part of multispecialty clinics, hospitals, or other large health-care organizations sometimes have a separate record system. That system, with appropriate confidentiality safeguards, should be accessible to the facility's emergency staff. Sometimes a clinician can be called on to provide critically relevant parts of the record without revealing extraneous material. (For additional discussion of confidentiality, see Chapter 9.)

When you return to your practice, whether the next morning or after a vacation, you should be available for feedback from the on-call professional; he or she may need to tell you something relevant to your patients and their treatment. If you are the on-call or crisis-intervention person, you have a duty to communicate important clinical information to the treating clinician, regardless of patient wish or consent, and to be certain that your message is received.

Do not equate constant personal availability with good care. The patient purchases some of your time, and your promise to work within the standard of care. Telling the patient that he or she may call you anytime, even at home, may sound good on the surface, but experienced therapists know this is unreasonable (and often countertherapeutic) for most clinical work. I usually tell psychotherapy trainees to limit after-hours calls severely (except when they are "on call"), and never to give their home telephone number. The therapist's convenience aside, after-hours calls (especially to the therapist's home) encourage various forms of acting out by patient and therapist. Not taking calls at home keeps the therapeutic work where it belongs: in clinical sessions. In addition, therapists' families are much better off when the therapists separate work from home life.

AGENCY, COMMUNICATION, AND THE PATIENT'S RIGHT TO EXPECT YOUR UNDIVIDED ATTENTION

As already discussed (Chapter 2) once a clinician–patient relationship is formed, you have a fiduciary duty to your patient. His or her interests must come first in all but a handful of circumstances (such as when the patient threatens you or someone else). The therapist's allegiance to an employer, contractee, payer (e.g., insurance company, MCO), or other organization is subordinate to the clinician–patient relationship and the patient's interest. You should tell the patient about any relationships, rules (such as MCO rules), contract stipulations, and the like that might reasonably be expected to limit the patient's care. Such disclosure is primarily for the patient's information and use in decision making; it does not generally decrease your duty to meet the standard of care.

If you believe that you have an employment, contractual, or other relationship that *does* decrease your duty to the patient, or if your contract or terms of employment appear to ask that of you, you should clarify the "agency" issue with someone who understands the relevant legal and professional/ethical issues, such as your malpractice insurance carrier, attorney, or professional organization ethics committee. Document your discussion in notes or a file memo; an exchange of letters with specific questions and answers is even better. Do not rely on advice from employers or contractees, since they have their own conflicts of interest. Discussion with an experienced colleague may help, but is no substitute for legal advice.

Financial conflict of interest is not limited to employers and contractees. All sources of payment for care create some conflict. Fee-for-service can provide an incentive for unscrupulous clinicians to treat unnecessarily. Capitation and other managed-care plans encourage less—or less appropriate—care than the patient may need. Insurance companies often require clinical summaries, and usually pay differently for different diagnoses and symptoms. Be honest with your patient, and also with yourself.

Forensic conflict of interest is discussed in Chapter 8.

TERMINATING CARE

Planned termination rarely causes allegations of negligence or other legal problems. When planned termination occurs before the "end" of treatment for some reason (e.g., one of the parties moves or becomes unavailable), an offer of referral or transfer to another competent clinician should be made. Termination for nonpayment was discussed earlier in this chapter.

Patients often terminate on their own, with or without notice. If the patient wishes to stop seeing you, the matter should be appropriately discussed to deal with countertherapeutic impulses and other reasons why termination may not be in his or her best interest. If the patient insists, an offer of referral or transfer should be made and carefully documented.

If the clinician has reason to believe that the patient is likely to be a danger to self or others, appropriate steps should be taken to protect the relevant party. This clinical duty exists, in my opinion, whether or not your particular state or federal jurisdiction has a "Tarasoff-like" case or statute. From a purely clinical/ethical viewpoint, a number of actions may meet your duty in specific cases, including continued treatment, warnings to potential victims, voluntary hospitalization, attempts at civil commitment, and notifying the police. None of these can be generically recommended for every circumstance; certain ones may be assumed to meet risk-management requirements in your state or setting (see Chapter 11).

Many patients quit treatment by simply not showing up for their appointments. When this occurs, reasonable attempts should be made to contact the patient and offer to discuss the situation and/or refer him or her to another clinician. Many authorities suggest a registered letter if you cannot reach the patient by telephone; I think other means are usually sufficient. In any event, one should be certain that the patient is not abandoned (see above and Chapter 3), even though the patient has decided to leave, and carefully document the process.

Occasionally, termination results because the patient has died. Even in the strictest psychoanalytic cases, a reasonable expression of sympathy and family support is appropriate, and highly recommended. One may wish to offer brief counseling to family members.

What if the patient has committed suicide or died under circumstance that may be perceived, deservedly or not, as the clinician's fault? Opinions vary, with some attorneys and malpractice carriers recommending against contacting the family. I disagree, and believe the best course is for the clinician to act naturally and sincerely (but not to become defensive or accept blame). If the family becomes accusatory, one may listen, or simply express sympathy and quietly withdraw. I recommend against any discussion of blame, whether of oneself or someone else. It is prudent to make notes of conversations, visits, and specific comments made by you or family members.

• 6

PRACTICE SETTINGS AND STYLES

THE LAW MAY vary from setting to setting or state to state but the general concept of duty of care does not. One thing that keeps one's professional duty consistent across different settings is the patient's reasonable expectation of certain parameters of care.[12] Another is the concept of professional ethics.

Ethics do not vary over different settings or jurisdictions. Truly new clinical situations (such as *in vitro* fertilization or the ability to keep people "alive" after their brains have ceased to function) may require careful consideration of what is morally and professionally right, but those who redefine ethics merely to fit different treatment settings or funding arrangements are simply wrong. I recommend that clinicians not allow such redefinitions to guide their patient care, even when they appear to come from authoritative sources.

■ ■ ■

---

[12] Some clinicians and authors call these expectations of certain parameters of care "patients' rights." I prefer to separate real constitutional and statutory rights from patient expectations (even expectations that create a professional duty) because to call them "rights" confuses and trivializes constitutional and legislative concepts. Unless codified in statute, a "patients' bill of rights," for example, refers only to what patients may expect in the setting in which it is conceived. It has no real meaning elsewhere, and thus does not, in my opinion, create a standard of care.

MANAGED CARE

Do not expect me to rant against managed care in this section, despite the fact that in our surveys managed-care organizations (MCOs) were singled out for complaints and forensic concerns far more than any other setting or topic. We'll stick to our goal of identifying and addressing legal and ethical issues in clinical practice. Many topics that are not limited to MCOs (e.g., confidentiality, record keeping, conflict of interest) are not addressed in detail here, but in broader sections or chapters elsewhere in this book.

Constraint on clinical practice is one of the most troublesome aspects of work in managed-care settings. For our purposes, the question is simply whether or not the constraints interfere with the clinician's duty to his or her patient. The number of duties and responsibilities is large, of course, but the principle is the same.

The law, in general, rarely allows clinicians to shift responsibility to a third party. Even doctors and therapists who are employed by, say, an HMO cannot shed the mantle of responsibility merely by saying, in effect, "The boss (or contract, policy, insurer, treatment protocol, closed formulary) made me do it." If you believe that you are being asked to practice outside the standard of care, then you should take steps (and document those steps in some way) to clarify what you are asked to do, disclose choices and conflicts to your patient(s), and stay within your duty to the patient. Remember, your first duty is to the patient, regardless of who pays you. Note also that the "standard of care" is not the MCO's standard or protocol. *The standard by which you will be judged in a lawsuit (or ethics hearing) is defined by clinicians, not MCOs or insurers (or even MCO clinicians).*

Once one understands the preceding paragraphs, questions about confidentiality, treatment choices, medical records, and the like in MCOs become clearer in principle, if not in practice. The main issue for many therapists becomes whether or not to demand adequate care for their patients, or whether or not to work for the MCO in the first place (assuming there are constraints; not all MCOs are bad).

■ ■ ■

PRACTICING IN RURAL OR ISOLATED SETTINGS

Many of us dream of living in the country or a small town,[13] within walking distance of the office, which is probably on a Waldenesque pond. Practicing there has some special considerations, however, for confidentiality, isolation, supervision, and available resources. Clinicians in small towns or other isolated settings are under less professional scrutiny than their city colleagues, and the dearth of comparisons may cause the public to afford them a bit more respect (although some people in rural areas are not impressed by effete psychological concepts).

Confidentiality and conflict of interest are common problems. Therapists rarely discuss their patients inappropriately, but the community often becomes aware that the person is being seen. It is especially important to screen, train, and monitor office employees, since they are, unfortunately, often a source of local gossip. When patients are less "anonymous," consider a bit more file security.

It is difficult to do intensive or psychoanalytic work when the patient and therapist often see each other outside therapy, especially when the patient is a local banker, teacher, or professional with whom one (or one's family) must have extratherapeutic relationships. I once knew a traditionally trained analyst who lived outside of town and, in spite of being a friendly fellow, refrained from accepting any social invitations, even for a small dinner, in the community. He did not want to color his patients' transferences or make them uncomfortable, and believed, perhaps rightly, that if he didn't decline all invitations equally, the community would soon figure out who his patients were. A Jungian analyst in the same town had no such compunctions, and seemed to get along fine. The same issue often arises in training programs and psychoanalytic institutes, of course; it is hard to say how many hours it adds to candidates' treatment.

Do not move to a small town to avoid your responsibilities; rural patients deserve the same standards of care and privacy as do those in other locations. Small-town doctors and therapists often enjoy a

---

[13] Of course, I was raised in Texas, not Manhattan, and still spend a lot of time in the country. If this isn't your dream, skip to the next paragraph.

comfortable sense of informality, but should watch for seemingly harmless boundary crossing. Think before buying that new car from a patient's family's dealership, or making a patients' restaurant your regular hangout. Patients need you to be their therapist, not their friend or customer.

Practicing Unusual, Controversial, or Easily Misunderstandable Subspecialties

The mental health professions are often creative in the ways in which they view and try to help their patients. Some of our routine, proven methods seem exotic to laypeople (e.g., hypnosis, gestalt techniques, ECT); others, which may be quite legitimate when used appropriately, are controversial even among clinicians. Any form of assessment or treatment one uses outside research settings should be well validated in the professional literature, not merely in self-serving pseudo-professional articles. Careful documentation is critical. If you believe that very special or "last-resort" techniques are indicated, get an independent second opinion, if at all feasible; document your decision-making process carefully; document your intentions and techniques; and make sure that the consent process is very clear.

All of the above assumes that both the treatment and the therapist's intent are in the patient's interest. You are responsible for recognizing whether or not your behavior is outside the standard of care. When it is substandard, no amount of documentation or consent is likely to justify it.[14]

"Alternative" Biological Treatments

If you don't have a license to practice medicine, most states forbid you to prescribe even over-the-counter medications. Years ago, pharmacists

---

[14] In general, consent alone is not sufficient to absolve clinicians of bad or ill-considered care. You are the expert, not the patient, and you are the one who carries out the care. You are not allowed to knowingly lead him or her to a poor decision.

had to be cautious with their advice to customers lest they be accused of "practicing medicine without a license." I am not aware of any recent case in which a nonphysician was successfully sued for recommending a homeopathic (herbal or very-low-dose nonprescription) remedy so long as the recommendation did not interfere with the patient's medical treatment or access to treatment. You are almost certainly outside the standard if you misdiagnose or fail to refer when you reasonably should have known better (or when you have represented to the patient that you are knowledgeable in that field).

Once a person has come to you for professional help, advice that would be permissible from the patient's friend or relative may well constitute "clinical practice" (or even "practicing medicine"). This means that you should not recommend St. John's wort for your significantly depressed patients without collaborating with a qualified psychiatrist; advise a borderline or schizophrenic patient to stop prescribed medications; or tout a naturopathic remedy to someone with anxiety or "fatigue" problems. The difference between such recommendations and acceptable (and often useful) proposals like "try eating less red meat" or "cut out caffeine" is sometimes unclear, but I suggest caution.

None of this means that you should not *discuss* such things with your patients, for example, if they come up in therapy or in a context of referral to a specialist. *Clinically recommending* is the point, even if it is merely the patient's perception that you recommended something. Can you get away with benign advice to a patient who has mild symptoms? Probably; but try to notice whether or not you rationalize it in some way, then consider the possibility that your rationalization really represents some form of countertransference or self-serving action (such as pleasing the patient or wanting to "prescribe"). One limited rule of thumb: If you feel reluctant to record your action routinely in the patient's chart, it's probably unwise.

■ ■ ■

Is it outside the standard or unethical per se to work for a company that rations care, limits care based on ability to pay, or makes money from others' misery? No. Competition and the profit motive are often associated with improvements in products and services. Is it outside the standard or unethical per se to practice outside the norm so long as it is in your patient's interest? No. Your patient's interest largely defines the ethic. But consult your "moral compass" often and be aware that the legal and ethical standards of care transcend the setting in which you work. Is it difficult to maintain the standard of care in some practice settings? Of course; but graduate school was difficult, too, and your patients are relying on you.

·7

CONSENT

LEGALLY VALID CONSENT has three necessary elements: knowledge, competence, and voluntariness. When consent is required, the absence of any one of these prevents it.

Knowledge refers to information, which should be as complete as is reasonable for the level of potential danger, benefit, or inconvenience involved (see "Informed Consent," below).

Competence refers to whether or not the patient is mentally able to make reasonable use of that information. Consent for different things requires different levels of competence, usually depending on the complexity of the issue to be considered. When the issue is simple, the threshold for competence is generally low even if the risk is high (cf., a mildly mentally retarded person who is judged competent to consent to a lifesaving amputation based on knowing that the choice is between dying and living without a limb).

Children are generally defined as incompetent for medical purposes until they reach a particular age, which varies by state. The legal age of consent for medical or psychotherapeutic procedures is often lower than that for drinking or voting. Sometimes "assent" is required of older children, in addition to consent by a parent or guardian.

Voluntariness implies that the decision to consent is free of coercion. Many forms of coercion are subtle, such as the possibility that a prisoner will be considered for parole if he or she participates in therapy, or an unspoken threat of commitment if a psychotic patient does not agree to "voluntary" hospitalization. Small rewards may not constitute coercion for nonincarcerated people. Competent adults are usually allowed to volunteer for reasonably safe research in return for some reward, such as money or free medical care. It is generally inappropriate to offer rewards for clinical (not research) consent.

In a few situations, coercion always is assumed to be present (e.g., prisoners' not being allowed to consent to reasonably safe drug experiments because they might perceive a possibility of early release or special privileges, even when no such reward is offered). Some procedures are considered so controversial or dangerous that patients are not allowed to consent to them at all, even when they arguably have a positive effect (e.g., donating a kidney for money, volunteering for castration in order to get out of prison).

Written Versus Oral

Note that it is not necessary that a consent be written and signed. Signatures and written forms are merely documentation of consent and/or the consent process; they are not the consent itself. Oral, undocumented consents are just as valid, but make poor evidence if proof is needed later. Other forms of documentation of the consent and consent process include having witnesses, making audiotape or video recordings, and writing a summary of oral consent in the clinical record soon after it occurs.

Informed Consent

The phrase "informed consent" is a little misleading, since information is only one of the three required elements. Nevertheless, providing sufficient information is a very important issue in the patient's agreement to do something with or for the therapist. "Informed" refers to all the information that is reasonably relevant to the patient's decision. It does not require every shred of available data or information that is so esoteric that it is unlikely to matter in the case at hand.

When the reasonableness of the information is being estimated, the likelihood of some effect on the patient should be balanced against the importance of that effect. When speaking of adverse effects of a treatment, for example, problems that are fairly rare but very dangerous should be included; those that are very common but benign should probably be mentioned; but those that are both rare and benign may be omitted. Consent and disclosure processes for surgical procedures are often codified by medical organizations. Those for medications follow rough rules related to known rates and severity of side effects. Standardized descriptions of risks are available for many medical and surgical procedures that reassure the clinician who is not sure how much to tell the patient. Unfortunately, there are few written standards for consent to psychiatric and psychotherapeutic procedures.

Physicians, especially, sometimes ask whether or not they must tell the patient about frightening but very rare adverse effects. There are situations in which the clinician truly believes that a patient's unreasonable fears would interfere with a rational decision, and in some of those cases, it is appropriate to keep some information about potential dangers from the patient. A psychiatrist, for example, may occasionally be justified in keeping information about tardive dyskinesia from a severely psychotic patient, if telling the patient would be likely to harm him or her by creating an unreasonable fear and thus refusal of medication. Such situations, however, must be very carefully considered, suggest that consultation and/or a second opinion may be prudent, and are almost unheard of in nonmedical psychotherapy.

Consent for nonmedical procedures, such as various forms of psychotherapy, is not as well defined as consent for specific medications or procedures. Known adverse effects should be considered for inclusion in a consent process. If a procedure or technique is particularly controversial, or recent legal cases suggest caution, there seems to be little reason not to explain it carefully before beginning.

OTHER FORMS OF CONSENT

Implied consent is that which may reasonably be assumed because a person (patient, in this case) accedes to a simple request, or does not protest when he or she could easily do so. It requires the same elements (knowledge, competence, voluntariness), but applied in such obvious situations that the elements may not be readily apparent. Implied consent is the most common form of consent, occurring every time a patient merely cooperates with a clinical procedure or request.

Expressed consent is that which is somehow asserted by the patient. It may be expressed orally, in writing, or in some other way.

Substituted consent is that which is provided by someone other than the patient, such as a parent, guardian, conservator, or court. The person who provides substitute consent must be legally entitled to do so.

EXPIRATION

Consent is not forever. Different forms of consent expire after shorter or longer periods of time. Consents for clinical treatment are generally in effect while the treatment continues, but expire soon after it ends or is interrupted. Many long-term psychiatric treatment programs renew patient consents for treatment or hospitalization yearly, although I am not aware of any particular legal case that mandates the practice. Continuing ordinary psychotherapy does not require reconsent, since (1) only implied consent is required in most cases and (2) participation itself is evidence and expression of consent. When treatment is not the patient's choice, such as when it is a probation requirement, documentation of the patient's motivation to continue is prudent.

ASSENT

Assent implies agreement but does not imply legal consent. Some state laws and organization (e.g., clinic) procedures require that a person who is not entitled to consent (such as a minor above a certain age) add his or her *assent* to the parent's or guardian's *consent*. Parents are usually authorized to force minors to obtain lifesaving treatment, but psychotherapy and psychiatric hospitalization often require assent if the child is over 12 or 13 years of age. Of course, it is difficult to carry out therapy without some level of assent.

■　■　■

ADVANCE DIRECTIVES

Deeply depressed or psychotic patients sometimes become incompetent to consent and/or irrationally refuse potentially helpful treatment. Most states have some mechanism by which patients can consider treatment while fully competent and provide a "directive" to future doctors in "advance" for such things as hospitalization, medication, or ECT. This form of consent should be written or videotaped. Since it is designed to be irrevocable by the patient when he or she is incompetent, it should be carried out under specific conditions, usually defined by state law. Advance directives are common in general medical practice (cf., living wills, "do not resuscitate" requests), and may be revoked at any time, so long as the patient is competent.

· 8

BOUNDARY VIOLATIONS

I DON'T ALWAYS LIKE the phrase "boundary violations." It is often misunderstood (or poorly defined), and can be used to lump a broad variety of behaviors that may be imprudent or improper into an amorphous category of assumed immorality. Many boundary violations are destructive, and some reprehensible; but not all are unethical or even countertherapeutic per se.

This chapter begins with the assumption that the reader is not knowingly engaged in the boundary violations described. Some of the recommendations that sound defensive are designed, instead, to eliminate the *appearance* of violations, since, fair or not, that appearance often gives rise to suspicion. Unless stated otherwise, the chapter will refer to adult, generally competent patients. Exploiting children, severely disabled patients, or otherwise clearly incompetent ones goes well beyond the concept of "boundary violation."

A. SEXUAL BOUNDARY VIOLATIONS

All major organizations of mental health professionals decry sexual activity with patients. Many include past patients in their prohibitions (i.e., activity that begins after they no longer are patients). Several states have passed statutes that make such behaviors specific causes of legal action, even crimes. The prohibitions often seem superficially clear, but may not define "sexual activity" very well. In addition, many statutes and, especially, ethical canons do not differentiate (1) brief behaviors from lasting, calculated, and/or predatory ones; (2) recent behavior from that which occurred decades ago; and (3) intense clinical relationships from one-time or brief consultations. Nevertheless, rigid requirements and interpretations are a fact of life for the present, and should lead clinicians to become highly aware of the rules of their profession and locale, and of their appearance to a sometimes accusing or suspicious public.

> An older clinician with an excellent reputation had a brief affair with a patient early in his career. He quickly felt remorse and took all the professional steps believed appropriate by his profession at the time of the transgression (e.g., took responsibility for his behavior, stopped treating her, referred her to another therapist, terminated the affair, and entered intensive psychotherapy himself). There was no indication of other sexual activity with patients (or former patients) for the remainder of his career.
>
> Some three decades later, as he was preparing to retire, the former patient contacted him and threatened to make the affair public if he did not pay her a large sum of money.[15] He declined and contacted the police, then admitted the incident to both his state licensing board and his professional organization.
>
> The police dealt with the former patient's extortion attempt (he did not press charges). The licensing board investigated and declined to take any action, citing the years that had passed without further problems, the actions he took to minimize damage to the patient and future patients, and his now-excellent reputation. However, his national professional organization, of which he had been an active member, expelled him, in spite of many colleagues' recommendations for less punitive action.

In most circumstances, stating that an adult, competent patient consented is not a defense (or not a very good one) to allegations of sexual impropriety. Various theories question a patient's opportunity or

---

[15] The possibility of extortion is yet another reason, albeit not the primary moral or ethical one, to avoid sexual behavior with patients.

capacity to consent adequately to sex with a therapist, including the fiduciary trust between clinician and patient, exploitation of transference feelings when the patient doesn't realize their true source, the right of the patient to expect *clinical* needs to be the doctor's top priority both now and in the future, exploitation of some patients' inability to resist the influence of the therapist, and—related but not identical—an alleged "power differential" between any patient and his or her clinician.

There is further reason to highlight immoral behavior by mental health clinicians and trainees. We are entrusted with extremely intimate information, and with the responsibility of helping patients correct their problems, not add to them. Every patient who shares these things with us, or who might do so in the future, deserves to be able to rely on both our moral and professional competence. Our ethical promise must go beyond even those of many physicians, especially when we form and work with intimate relationships, in private, over long periods. We are susceptible to our own internal foibles, conscious and unconscious, which, if not controlled, can quickly place the patient in jeopardy.

Clinicians sometimes cite doctors or therapists who have married a patient. Laudable or not, I know of no case in which a clinician has been sued or prosecuted for actually marrying a patient who was unmarried during treatment (which used to happen far more often than it does today). Breaking up a patient's marriage is another matter.

A clinician left his wife for a current therapy patient, who was herself married. They eventually married. The former patient's ex-husband filed charges of "criminal conversation" (based on a state law against one person's sabotaging the marriage of another), and the clinician eventually lost his license.

It seems reasonable to assume that a prior clinical relationship would be a serious problem in any future divorce proceedings, but I have no data on the subject. It is clear, however, that a nonmarital relationship with a former patient has a considerable chance of ending with a lawsuit or an accusation of unethical behavior.

AVOIDING THE OPPORTUNITY FOR ACCUSATIONS

Several respondents to our survey of counselors and therapists decried their vulnerability to allegations of boundary violations should they touch patients in any way. At least one risk-management training video warns against even touching a grieving patient's shoulder, saying that it could lead to undue familiarity. I disagree with that particular recommendation, and believe that clinical common sense, with adequate documentation, usually allows appropriate expressions of sympathy and empathy without much fear of criticism. Be alert, however, to the fact that minor boundary violations (e.g., lending bus fare or failing to discuss the therapeutic implications of a small Christmas gift) sometmes evolve into later, major ones. Similarly, investigations of severe violations regularly reveal an earlier, escalating series of less serious ones.

Paranoia aside, some actions have the *appearance* of being unwise. Coincidental or not, several of the following frequently appear in lawsuits involving sexual allegations. Note that the use of feminine pronouns does not erase the fact that at least 5–10% of improper sexual behavior occurs between female therapists and male patients, and some between those of the same sex.

Things Commonly Viewed as "Red Flags" in Ethics Actions or Lawsuit Petitions

- Avoiding documentation of incidents or parts of the treatment that reasonable therapists would be expected to note in the chart (e.g., not mentioning gifts, telephone calls to or from the patient, or sexual material, or the clinical discussion they should generate). It is difficult to convince others that something is routine if it appears to have been hidden from the record.
- Seeing patients of the opposite sex alone in a deserted clinic or office, especially during odd or evening hours.
- Changing session hours or meeting circumstances to such a setting without documenting a good reason.
- Seeing patients alone in their homes, or yours.

- Avoiding supervision, consultation, or documentation with one or two female patients when such activities are routine for other patients.
- Locking the office door during therapy sessions.

Less Often Criticized, But Sometimes Cited

- Nonroutine calling of a patient by her first name, and/or vice versa, without considering its therapeutic implications.
- Suddenly engaging in particularly frequent, intensive, and/or private therapy that is not usually associated with one's professional training or clinical style.
- Telling office staff in some unusually vigorous way not to disturb the therapy session, such as berating a staff member for knocking on or opening the therapy office door.
- Having sexually suggestive artwork or materials visible to patients. (There is, of course, no reliable definition for "suggestive.")
- Being known as a "sex therapist" or a clinician who focuses on sexual problems.
- Talking a lot about a sexual topic when it was not the patient's primary complaint.
- Being a male therapist with a large caseload of women with marital or relationship problems.

Many (but not all) of the above behaviors are usually innocent. Some may be clinically indicated, routine, or merely a matter of therapist style. Some are necessary to accommodate patients' schedules or to develop a competitive practice when the daytime markets are saturated. Therapists should be aware, though, as a practical matter, that their behaviors may at some point be questioned by lawyers and juries, and should be alert to the possibility of their own rationalization and denial when they treat some patients as "special."

Recording therapy sessions solely to defend against accusations has never seemed a good idea to me. It has its proponents, and various reasons for recording therapy have waxed and waned in popularity over the years. I suppose there are settings in which it may be indicated, but in general, to record for such an obviously defensive reason adds a non-therapeutic dimension to an activity that I believe should focus on clinical issues, not future accusation potential. It makes a bit more sense to record trainee sessions, or those of clinicians who are in some type of probationary or supervisory period. Recording creates documentation, and some may feel that it is an extra "conscience." On the other hand, practitioners who choose to record their sessions may be the ones least likely to transgress.

If you do choose to record sessions, be certain that the patient consents to both the recording and the method of storage for the tapes, and audibly document the date and time of each session. Storing tapes in the office is one option. For additional security and credibility, one can engage a service (now available in many cities) that will set up automatic, tamper-resistant equipment and store the used audio- or videotapes off-site, warranting them to be unaltered and confidential until unsealed by an appropriate authority.

OFFICE HOURS, LOCATIONS, CHAPERONES

Experienced therapists know that the easiest hours to fill are often early, late, lunchtime, or on Saturdays. Those times are convenient for patients who work, and are logical "moonlighting" hours for therapists who have daytime salaried jobs. Therapists with part-time practices, such as those who work on their own after regular job hours, are more likely than others to use home offices or other places that lack secretaries, receptionists, and other office personnel. While there is nothing inherently wrong with this, such locations, like irregular hours, lend themselves to doubts when added to accusations of improper behavior.

Having said that there is nothing wrong with unusual hours or locations per se, it is important to add that the *reasons* for them can either support or refute an allegation of impropriety. Why has a male therapist chosen to see an attractive female patient when no one else is in the office suite? Why have regular afternoon appointments suddenly been changed to 6:00 P.M., after the receptionist has gone home? Changes in time or setting generally raise more concerns than do the initial choices.

A therapist was accused of having an affair with a patient at a mental health center. One of the points of contention was the fact that he had changed the site of her therapy from a central clinic to a more isolated rural one. The ensuing lawsuit alleged that he saw her during lunch hours and in the late afternoon (although review of the appointment schedule suggested that this was not the case), often encouraging the lone receptionist to go to lunch or leave for the day while the patient was still there. The case was settled for an unknown amount.

Many things besides time and location can predispose a therapy setting to boundary violations. Sometimes a patient wants to set up a special treatment *environment,* to create the feeling (or the reality) that the clinician *relationship* is also "special." Therapists, particularly men, may be consciously or unconsciously susceptible to such seductions,[16] which are more common with some diagnoses than with others. One should be alert to impulses of either therapist or patient to seek out a potentially troublesome treatment circumstance.

Training programs and large clinics have a duty to be aware of potential problems among trainees and employees. The credentialing process deals with part of the duty, but there may be a responsibility to monitor treatment environments and scheduling for some clinicians (particularly trainees or those on some form of probation). In my opinion, accepted standards of care and clinic management do not require the monitoring of ordinary clinicians' scheduling and offices when there is no reasonable suspicion of improper behavior.

Responsibility for Reporting

Most state professional boards (particularly those that license psychologists and physicians) have some requirement that licensees report colleagues reasonably suspected of sexual activity with patients. The mandate may be part of rules about reporting clinicians

---

[16] "Seduction" is used here, and often elsewhere in this book, in its psychodynamic sense, and does not necessarily imply sexual impulses or behaviors.

who are not practicing safely and competently, or be included in a specific rule regarding sexual behavior.

Several states have passed strict reporting laws in addition to licensing/certifying board rules. The most stringent require that if any patient mentions, even in passing, a past sexual relationship with a doctor or therapist to a *current* clinician, the current one must report it to the appropriate licensing authority (and, in a few cases, a law enforcement agency). In at least one state, the report must be made regardless of whether or not the patient wishes to keep it private.

Be certain you understand your state's reporting requirements for your profession, and follow them. Any disagreement you may have with them, such as about reporting a distant past event when the patient asks you not to, should be treated as any other legal dissent: first comply, then pursue whatever disagreement you may have.

B. NONSEXUAL BOUNDARY VIOLATIONS[17]

TRYING TO "HELP" PATIENTS BY USING INAPPROPRIATE DIAGNOSIS OR DISHONEST REPORTS OR RECORDS

We discussed this common boundary violation in earlier chapters. While it may appear to be in the patient's interest to give a diagnosis that qualifies him or her for reimbursement, hospitalization, or disability payments, or even to testify falsely on a patient's behalf in a legal matter, it is unethical and illegal to do so. In addition, such behavior moves outside the clinician–patient relationship to become a "special favor," and communicates countertherapeutic messages of dishonesty. In a worst-case scenario, the patient can turn the dishonesty or fraud

---

[17] This section is not intended to criticize some "case management" activities, such as those commonly seen in social support or "assertive community treatment" programs for severely and chronically mentally ill patients, or in planned and documented inpatient or residential psychosocial programs. Such efforts should be separated from the concept of clinician–patient psychotherapy relationships (and are usually performed by different people). Of course, staff members of these programs can overstep *their* boundaries with sexual or other behaviors.

into a tool for therapist blackmail. (This is also true of sexual boundary violations, even years after the imprudent behavior.)

When an insurance company or disability agency requests copies of your existing records, for example, to update their files regarding the patient, you should comply so long as the patient authorizes release of the information. It is prudent to tell the patient what information will be released and to discuss the possible consequences. It is *not* appropriate to "collude" with the patient to create inaccurate or misleading information for the third party.

If your patient is not currently receiving insurance or government benefits but may deserve them, you may suggest that he or she consider applying, so long as your intent is to help the patient, and not to increase your own income. I believe it is generally inappropriate for the treating clinician to perform the primary disability assessment, although one certainly may supply copies of your records, diagnosis, and so on, for the agency's evaluation.

ACCEPTING FINANCIAL GAINS BEYOND REASONABLE FEE OR EXCHANGE

It may be unethical to accept significant gifts or compensation outside the routine fee for your services. Accepting a small gift may be harmless, but may also indicate (or portend) an inappropriate relationship with or expectation by the patient. It is a therapeutic truism that patients do not give gifts without wanting something in return, and that the symbolism involved in the gift (whether or not it is accepted) should be discussed whenever there is a close therapeutic relationship.

Substantial gifts of gratitude usually should be gently declined. Psychoanalyst Harry Stack Sullivan said it well: the only reward to which the therapist is entitled is the fee. Sullivan was also referring to whether or not therapists should allow themselves personal gratification from their patients' successes.

Handmade gifts are often treated differently from purchased ones. It may be countertherapeutic to decline something the patient has produced himself or herself, unless it is quite valuable. Discussion, placing the gift in a therapy-related context, and documentation are all keys to dealing with the potential boundary issues. Incidentally, I suggest that one not destroy such gifts when they are accepted, and when feasible, it may be a good idea to file them with the patient's record.

When gifts are used as evidence of financial impropriety or undue influence, courts often consider whether or not the clinician directly benefited from the gift. Donations to the therapist's favorite charity are different from becoming a beneficiary of a changed will or accepting a new Mercedes. Still, ethics charges may be brought in some cases.

> An elderly patient told his psychoanalyst that he planned to leave him a substantial bequest. The clinician recommended against the action, and encouraged extensive exploration of the patient's wish and underlying motivation. When the patient died several years later, his will provided a substantial gift for a nonprofit clinical institution of which the analyst was an officer. The analyst had not been aware of the change in the former patient's will, the bequest did not benefit him directly, and, after some consideration, he recommended that the institution accept the money.
>
> The former patient's children, whose inheritances were much decreased by the gift, alleged that the analyst had unduly influenced their father and sued to recover the gift. The institution settled the suit, but the analyst was charged by his professional association with violating ethical canons, and was eventually expelled.

"INSIDE INFORMATION"

A corollary of "undue influence" is the situation in which one attempts to benefit from profitable "inside information," such as investment information, since that could constitute a substantial gift and/or affect the treatment. Even if one hears of such things coincidentally, acting to benefit oneself may be unethical. For example, if a patient who is a company executive divulges some business matter during therapy that might affect the price of a stock, buying or selling the stock could be considered a breach of privilege, an action in other than the patient's interest, or insider trading.

The same applies to help or "tips" you might give to the patient. Your usefulness to patients lies in your clinical skills and your separation of your professional role from other roles better found elsewhere in their lives. Do not suggest, recommend, or even inform the patient concerning such things as investments, and be cautious about direct advice on such topics as employment and relationships. There is a difference between eliciting thoughts and feelings to encourage good decision making and inappropriately influencing those decisions. (This does not imply that the therapist should support a patient's destructive, illegal, or clearly immoral [and thus likely destructive] behavior. Omitting appropriately phrased criticism of such behaviors is rarely in the patient's interest.)

▪ 9

CONFIDENTIALITY AND PRIVILEGE

PRIVILEGE IS THE *Patient's Right* to keep protected information confidential. Confidentiality is the *Clinician's Obligation* to abide by that privilege.[18] The privilege belongs to the patient, not to the clinician. With certain exceptions, the privilege is automatically asserted in the patient's name, and waiver requires some action on his or her part.

EXCHANGING INFORMATION WITH OTHER PROFESSIONALS

There is generally no need to worry about authorization when exchanging information with other clinicians in the patient's interest. The therapist's duty to inform other clinicians when necessary to protect the patient's well-being should not be limited by absence of patient authorization. Note that information that is not relevant to the other clinician's care of the patient should not be released without authorization.

One does not need a release to provide clinically relevant feedback to a colleague who has referred the patient for consultation or to provide summary information when referring the patient oneself.

---

[18] This clever reminder (PRivilege and COnfidentiality) first came to me from Dr. Thomas Gutheil.

Accepting a referral for ongoing treatment, however, does not entitle the referrer to further information gained unless it is clearly important to the other clinician's care.

Nonclinicians who refer patients, such as friends, relatives, employers, or teachers, are not entitled to feedback without release, unless there is a significant protection-of-others issue (e.g., workplace safety) or you have some form of dual agency with, say, an employer or school that requires reporting. In the first case, the various states have differing requirements and exemptions for disclosing danger to self or others; be familiar with those in your state (and see Chapters 10 and 11). In the second, be sure to disclose your dual agency to the patient at the outset.

GIVING INFORMATION TO FAMILY MEMBERS

Family members sometimes request information about, especially, a spouse's or child's therapy. They are often concerned about the patient, and may be very frustrated by release procedures that you see as necessary and routine.

When the patient is an adult, he or she generally controls the release of ordinary information to the family, even when some other family member is paying for the therapy. In my opinion, this general rule may be carefully broken in some circumstances; such as when there is good reason to suspect danger to self or others, when considering civil commitment, or when the need is great and you suspect that the patient is not capable of understanding the release authorization process (see "Getting Information from Others," below).

Minors' records are usually available to a parent or guardian (but be cautious with a noncustodial parent who may have no right to the information, even if he or she brought the child to you in the first place). Adolescents may have certain rights to privilege in some states, usually beginning around age 16. It is wise to discuss limitations on confidentiality with both the parents and the young patient at the beginning of treatment. You may have policies about informally keeping a child's confidences, with a broadly understood intent to keep his or her comments private; however, do not promise that "everything you say will be confidential." When the child's safety or other important interests are at stake, bring the parents into the picture. If you are concerned that parental discussion may lead to child abuse or other harm by one or both parents, a conference with the safe parent (if any) and child-protection authorities is in order. Do not allow a misguided view of the child's privilege, which largely belongs to the parent or guardian, to interfere with your duty to protect him or her from harm.

GETTING INFORMATION FROM OTHERS

Failure to obtain important historical information from corroborating sources is a common precursor of negligence allegations. The standard does not generally require extensive history before ordinary psychotherapy, but inpatient admission or assessment of severe or potentially dangerous symptoms generates a duty to gather a comprehensive history and to seek corroboration of the clinical and social background as required for accurate diagnosis and safe treatment. When assessing a psychotic, disoriented, or morbidly depressed patient, for example, talking with the family or others is often necessary to assess suicide risk or behavior, other violence, exposure to toxic substances, and the like.

In such a situation, one should try to get authorization to disclose the fact that the patient is receiving care. If the patient refuses permission, one should carefully weigh the pros and cons of seeking the information anyway. Although confidentiality is very important, you also have a duty to act in the patient's best interest. There are at least four concepts that often suggest contacting a relevant outside person (or persons): (1) You cannot carry out your fiduciary duty to the patient without the best available clinical and psychosocial information, and that duty arguably transcends some of your obligation of confidentiality. (2) The patient may not be competent to decide whether or not to authorize contact with others and/or to decide what is in his or her best interest. In such cases, it may be sufficient to document your impression that the patient is incapable of rationally refusing reasonable authorization; however, a second opinion is recommended. Many attorneys would suggest seeking a court order or finding of incompetence. (3) There may be an emergency in which the patient's life or limb (including mental "limb") depends on rapid, accurate information. (4) It is usually much easier to defend a lawsuit for negligent release of information than one for negligent assessment or diagnosis that leads to severe damage to the patient or others.

Unless the patient can reasonably allege severe damage due to a breach of privilege, a lawsuit would seem unlikely. Although acting outside the confidentiality standard in this way might occasionally be grounds for censure by one's professional organization, licensing body, or health-care employer, the "good faith" nature of one's actions seems important to the defense.

It is important to note that I did not refer to authorization to release any information *except the fact that the patient is receiving care.* When a family member or friend is clearly aware that the patient is receiving care (e.g., when it was he or she who brought the patient to the hospital or clinic in the first place), disclosure of that fact would not seem to be a legal issue. Thus the clinician should be able to ask questions and listen to the answers without revealing information about the patient, in a sort of "one-way" flow of communication *to* but not *from* the clinician.[19]

RELEASE AUTHORIZATION[20]

The authorization for release of information is a consent, and requires that the elements of consent be met (knowledge, competence, and voluntariness; see Chapter 7). Like other consents, it can be rescinded by a competent patient at any time. Otherwise it expires at some point, such as when noted on the form (usually 60 days to a year after signing), when specified by statute, or at some time determined by a court if the consent is contested.

---

[19] Although I have recommended this technique to hospital psychiatrists for years, I am not aware of any legal case that establishes that it does not constitute "release of information." Breach of privilege is rarely the primary allegation in negligence or malpractice lawsuits.

[20] The word "patient," as used here, when referring to the person who authorizes release (or rescinds that authorization), includes legally authorized parents and guardians.

Content

It is wise to include a number of things on the release form, although if the contents are not specified in statute, the written form merely documents the consent, and is not the authorization per se. Clinical employers and health-care organizations often have specific policies covering the content and format of release authorizations. Forms often include, but may not be limited to, the date, identifying data, a reasonably specific description of the kind of information to be released, and the specific person(s), entity(ies), or kind of person/entity entitled to receive it. There may be a comment that the patient understands what he or she is signing, and has had an opportunity to have the form explained (or has had it explained) in detail. An expiration date is common, but not generally required, and may refer not to a particular date but to something like "while a patient at _____ Hospital." It is wise to note that although the patient may rescind the authorization at any time, the recission does not apply to information that has already been released in good faith.

Validity and Expiration

A hospital authorization for release of information is routinely valid for at least the entire admission (almost always less than the term on the form), particularly for purposes of talking with family members or payers. It may be considered invalid for some purposes after discharge, even if the hospitalization only lasts a few days, and may be used for such things as documenting care for payment purposes or sending clinical information to professionals with a "need to know."

In office practice, it is often prudent to renew releases for special reports or communications (e.g., disability reports) every time a new need arises, but this is probably not legally necessary if the release has not expired and the material released was reasonably anticipated in the original authorization. Releases for insurance company payment or general communication need not be renewed so often, provided one adheres to the printed expiration notice and statutory maximums.

Prospective release refers to the release of information that is obtained after the authorization is signed. It is routine, and within the standard in my opinion, to release such information in good faith unless prohibited from doing so on the authorization form or by some special statute. Common examples include reports to payers and communication to family members about treatment progress.

SUBPOENAS AND DISCLOSURE

The basic principle here is, "Never ignore a subpoena." On the other hand, not all subpoenas are from courts and judges; some are merely from attorneys. Many of these contain unreasonable requests that can be successfully challenged on the basis of irrelevance, privilege, or being unduly onerous. Nevertheless, some response is mandatory, which leads to the next principle: Contact your lawyer for advice.

When you are subpoenaed to appear or testify about your clinical work with a patient (and assuming you are a fact, not expert, witness; see Chapter 2), you probably will have to appear before the judge or at deposition. The most common format in such cases is a *subpoena duces tecum,* which demands that you appear and bring all your records of the case (including financial records). Local subpoenas for fact witnesses have geographic limits. If you insist on avoiding them (which I don't recommend; it's a lot of trouble), there is some defined distance you must travel to get beyond the court's reach.

DO NOT give original patient records to anyone (although certain kinds of subpoenas or search warrants in criminal cases, such as Medicaid or Medicare fraud investigations, may entitle law enforcement officers to take your records as evidence). Subpoenas or other legal requests may entitle the recipient to verify that the entire record is properly copied. This can usually be accomplished by having someone witness the copying or sending the chart to a professional legal copy service (seek instructions from your malpractice carrier or lawyer). Don't let a patient's lawyer to do the copying, and don't allow anyone other than a neutral legal copy service remove records from your office.

■ ■ ■

SOME COMMON MISUNDERSTANDINGS
ABOUT THE PRIVACY OF YOUR PATIENT RECORDS

- **The patient's intimate revelations are absolutely confidential (privileged).** This is just not true. There are several circumstances, albeit rare and often extreme, that create an opportunity, and sometimes a duty, to divulge what has transpired in the therapy. One is the patient's competent demand that you do so. Others include lawful subpoenas and protection of others (e.g., children in child abuse cases). You should not say, or imply, to the patient that what he or she says is absolutely confidential.

- **Therapists can refuse to supply detailed records of assessment or treatment when they believe it violates their ethics or the patient's best interest.** Although you may picture yourself as a righteous martyr, going to jail for refusing the demands of some misunderstanding judge, the fact is that when the court is entitled to your information, your protests quickly begin to appear self-serving rather than truly based on patient-care principles. Sometimes the information can be revealed to the judge in private (*in camera*).

- **Although the main patient records may be released, with authorization or for some other legal reason, the court and lawyers are not entitled to "private" therapy or psychoanalytic notes.** The record is the record, and includes private or "process" notes that are not kept with the main file. Keeping a second, more private set of notes may be a good idea to protect the patient's revelations from the prying eyes of secretaries, medical records personnel, or other clinicians; however, the second set is no more privileged than the main file when your record is subpoenaed. Do not attempt to hide the private notes.

- **Raw psychological test data do not have to be released, even with authorization or subpoena.** Some professional organization ethics demand that psychologists never divulge raw test data to anyone other than a qualified clinician. In my opinion, this *organization* guideline has little or no standing to combat a lawful subpoena or patient release in *legal* settings unless state statute awards some of the patient's privilege to the therapist.

Psychologists occasionally argue that, contrary to the truism that "the privilege (of confidentiality) belongs to the patient," their states' laws allow clinicians to own some of the privilege. I know of no cases, however, in which a court has ruled that a psychologist need not divulge test data.

DISCLOSURE TO PAYERS

When patients purchase health insurance or join a health plan, they routinely sign an authorization for release of information to the payer. Even though the release is signed well in advance of diagnosis and treatment, it is considered valid, often for several years (as long as the policy is in effect). In some cases, the insurer's release statement specifies only information required to process the claim for payment; in others, it is a blanket release for any information the payer may request. Even when it appears to be "legal," clinicians should be cautious about revealing material not reasonably needed for payment.

Therapists concerned about confidentiality and payers—including insurers, managed-care organizations, and employer-financed programs—should remember that the patient agreed to reasonable information release when he or she signed the contract. Patients have a choice, in that they are welcome to decline insurance reimbursement and thus avoid any release of information.[21]

[21] This has only recently become true, in a very limited way, for patients over 65, and is still being contested in Congress. If the therapist participates in Medicare, the patient's records for covered procedures are vulnerable to survey by the Health Care Financing Administration (HCFA) even if Medicare is not billed. Certain clinicians may opt out of the Medicare system if the patient agrees to waive his or her right to federal Medicare benefits (for the psychotherapy only; other benefits are not affected). The rules are complex, and currently require the clinician to opt out of all Medicare reimbursement, for all patients. Confidentiality protections for senior citizens were the impetus for this "private contracting" legislation, which may become less rigid in the future.

· 10

SUICIDE AND OTHER DANGER TO SELF

OUR PURPOSE HERE is not to examine exhaustively the many clinical and risk factors associated with suicidal patients, patients who talk about suicide, and those with self-destructive behaviors. Instead, we focus on several topics specific to clinician liability.

AWARENESS

"Awareness" is different from "prediction"; we can argue about predictability, but you have a clear duty to recognize reasonable signs of suicide risk. Although standards for and types of diagnosis and treatment vary among the mental health professions (from psychiatry to pastoral counseling, for example), when it comes to self-destructive behaviors, every clinician and therapist is expected to recognize patient danger. The attorney knows that juries pay great attention to tragedy, such as a family left bereft by the death of its breadwinner, and want to blame someone for what they often believe—rightly or wrongly—is an "unfair" outcome.

■ ■ ■

Assessment

You must do some form of initial assessment before beginning even the most superficial counseling. Pastoral, educational, and marriage and family counselors are among those who often neglect this step, since their patients/clients often seem healthy and their problems appear focused rather than broad. Nevertheless, these professionals, too, are expected to (1) take an adequate history, (2) perform a relatively comprehensive introductory interview (i.e., broader and more comprehensive than later focused counseling sessions), and (3) monitor the patient(s) for signs of worsening, misdiagnosis, or a new diagnosis. At each step, you must be able to recognize reasonable warning signs. The standard for recognition varies somewhat with your profession, but, if a tragedy occurs, your actions will be scrutinized in a very emotional, sometimes completely nonclinical, context.

Each profession's assessment standard is different. All other things being equal, psychiatrists have the most complex duty. The setting in which the assessment takes place is much less important; do not think that your crowded schedule or managed-care limitations on the evaluation (time or reimbursement) will be an adequate hedge against liability.

Protecting the Patient

You are not responsible for your patient's life. You *are* responsible for trying to help your patient and remaining within the standard of care. If you do, fewer patients will die by their own hand. If you do not, on average, more will die. Thus your deviation from the standard increases, to a lesser or greater extent, the *probability* that a tragedy will occur. In a lawsuit, the plaintiff must prove, by a preponderance of the evidence, that your deviation from the standard *caused* it. This is often interpreted (properly or not) as "but for" causation; that is, but for your deviation, the tragedy would not have occurred. It's that simple.

After proper assessment and recognition of suicide risk, your duty moves to protecting the patient. There are several ways to discharge that duty. Whether or not you do specific things is less important than whether or not you *consider* the relevant possibilities and make a decision based on reasonable factors. The worst criticisms come from lack of consideration of, and failure to document, a reasonable clinical thought process, not from your good-faith decision itself.

- When risk is high, act to protect the patient from immediate danger.

   Such actions include attempts to hospitalize (e.g., involuntarily) and calling family (or friends, in some cases) to discuss protecting the patient. Actions that involve only patient behavior or willpower (e.g., nonsuicide "contracts" or promises, or therapist instructions, such as cognitive-behavioral advice) will probably not be seen as sufficient in a lawsuit environment. After all, the patient is the one who wants to die. The illness, poor judgment, or misunderstanding of reality that drives serious suicide risk is usually a bigger factor in his or her life than promises to, or instructions from, the therapist.

- Consider consultation with a senior or specialized colleague.

- Consider referring the patient to someone or some entity that is better equipped to deal with the problem.

   It is important to consider protecting the patient during the referral process, including, for example, the trip from your office to a hospital. While it may seem logical to allow family or friends to take the patient to a psychiatrist or emergency room, remember that they are not mental health professionals, nor are they usually prepared to assume custody in the same way as are trained hospital or emergency staff.

Late one evening, a couple brought their adult son to a mental health crisis clinic after finding him contemplating suicide with a gun. A clinic counselor evaluated the patient, and then told the parents to take him to a nearby hospital. The counselor's notes indicated that she believed that the patient was acutely suicidal, and had called the emergency room to be sure that he would be seriously considered for admission. The parents were given no warnings or instructions, however, other than directions to the emergency room.

On the way, the young man jumped out of his parents' car, ran away in a darkened parking garage, and leaped to his death from the garage roof. The counselor and clinic were sued for failing to protect the patient. The facts that (1) he had been accepted for evaluation/care, (2) he was diagnosed as acutely dangerous to himself before being "released" to his parents, and (3) the counselor did nothing to help the parents keep him safe during transport were all raised in the plaintiffs' case.

• Once the patient is being protected (e.g., is in a protective environment such as a hospital), begin treatment and management techniques likely to decrease the risk rapidly and substantially.

This might include corroboration of the history, and such treatments as ECT or some rapidly acting medications, administered in an atmosphere of close monitoring ("suicide precautions"). Note that these treatments often cannot be provided by a nonmedical therapist; referral to a psychiatrist is usually necessary. Treatments that take longer to become effective, such as psychotherapy and many medications, are harder to justify for emergency use (and less likely to meet the standard of care), particularly if the patient is not well protected in the interim.

An unfamiliar suicidal patient requires an assessment that is as extensive as is reasonably feasible, including corroboration of the history and patient statements by available family or other persons. Do not neglect, for example, the person who brought the patient to the hospital or who found him or her in a suicidal setting. Treatment may, of course, begin while the comprehensive workup continues.

AFTER SUICIDE HAS OCCURRED

Most therapists experience at least one patient suicide during their careers. After any tragedy or adverse occurrence, one should communicate and express sympathy. Don't press yourself on the family, but do express support. Something like, "We did everything we could," is fine, if you can say it confidently and without sounding self-serving. Some supervisors recommend offering an informal session to the family without charge.

I believe that attending the funeral, if done as a genuine expression of respect for the patient or family, is appropriate in some situations. In others, it is not. Would you have attended if the patient had died in an accident? Were you invited by a member of the family (in which case, you should probably attend)? Has any member of the family asked you *not* to attend (in which case, you should probably honor that wish).

Some therapists are prone to unburdening themselves of feelings of doubt, guilt. or inadequacy in such situations, *even when those feelings have no real basis in the patient's actual care*. Others seek to make the family members feel better by taking on some of their potential for guilt. Still others, if they recognize that the family's religious beliefs (such as that suicide is a mortal sin) are making it hard to accept suicide, offer them solace by subtly shifting blame toward themselves or other factors. This is magnanimous but inaccurate (assuming you were not negligent), and statements made in any of these contexts can be very damaging later, if litigation ensues. Do not shrink from contact with and support for the family, but make sure that your contact focuses on that support, and not something else:

- Listen, don't talk. This is their time. If you need support or to unburden yourself, do it with a colleague or supervisor.[22]
- Be fairly cautious about the things you say and how you say them. Don't assume responsibility for, or even discuss your role in, the patient's behavior. Keep the conversation on the family's loss and grief.
- Don't allow yourself to be pulled into a discussion of the patient's care, especially around the time of death. This is not the time, and your comments can easily be misconstrued later.
- Don't second-guess your—or anyone else's—clinical actions.
- Don't second-guess the family's actions either. Once again, this is not the time.

---

[22] Consider doing it with your own counselor or therapist, since this creates a therapist–patient relationship and a privilege of confidentiality that is likely not to be discoverable. If, however, you are asking for clinical comment or guidance rather than personal help, it is really consultation or supervision and should be labeled as such.

- Don't blame the patient (although you may listen quietly to family comments about patient blame or behavior).
- Don't offer to forgive the bill. Your work was and is legitimate and proper. To discount or modify your charges at this time doesn't suggest only charity, but also guilt. Carry on the office business with reasonable routine (although you may wish to postpone the bill for a short time).
- Don't charge for the time you spend at funeral or memorial services (it's happened). Consider not charging for a brief session with the family, but I suggest charging routinely if your involvement with them goes beyond one meeting.
- Don't be false, cold, or self-serving. If, for some reason, you have trouble offering genuine support or empathy, just be there silently.
- Don't avoid the family. Take their calls and be reasonably available for support.
- Be aware that family members may express many different feelings. Don't take them all personally, and don't assume that either compliments or criticisms are all heartfelt or lasting. Don't explain your clinical actions, and don't become defensive.
- If the family's requests (or even the tone of communication) suggest criticism of your care, call your malpractice carrier at once and listen carefully to the representative's advice.

Some supervisors and attorneys recommend that the clinician jot down what family members say about the patient's care at supportive sessions (or even at funerals). I suppose that it may be helpful at trial to remind a suing relative that he or she complimented the clinician just after the death. On the other hand, such notes often sound self-serving (see below), and, in most cases, family members will simply (and sometimes rightly) say that they didn't know at the time what mistakes the therapist made, and weren't capable of recognizing the bad care.

Take good notes if you meet formally with family members, but do it routinely, just as you would for any other session. Lengthy, detailed notes of such sessions often sound self-serving when they are very different from your regular documentation style. (Note that this means you should already have a good documentation style.)

"Self-serving" Notes

I suggest that clinicians write a careful chart note soon after the patient's death that documents their clinical view of the situation. Some attorneys or carriers recommend against this, believing that therapists are likely to include, consciously or subtly, their own emotional concerns in the heat of the moment, or that such notes appear self-serving. However, since almost anything you write after a patient's death, especially a suicide, can be painted as "self-serving" by a plaintiff's lawyer, it seems to me that such notes, when they fill a clinical documentation need, are helpful more often than not. They will be a valuable *contemporaneous* record, more likely to help than hinder if there is a later question about the patient's condition, behavior, or care.[23] Write the note in a professional way, as a means of documenting the clinical facts while they are fresh in your mind (after all, you wouldn't wait days or weeks to write an ordinary progress note). Avoid personal or defensive comments; use your usual style as best you can without sounding cold or detached.

"Psychological Autopsies"

Our professions value professional discussion and feedback about our care, especially when things go wrong. It is an unfortunate fact, however, that today's risk-management climate demands great caution with any "psychological autopsy" unless one knows for certain that it is conducted in a highly protected (e.g., medical peer review) setting. Get advice from your hospital or clinic counsel or malpractice carrier before proceeding (such advice may be codified in larger institutions' or agencies' policy and procedure manuals). Do not assume that the mere fact that the discussion is formal, or with professionals, protects it from future discovery.

---

[23] It is a legal truism that what you remember and document at the time of an event is more accurate than what you try to recall months or years later (e.g., after a suit is filed, or at trial). This concept is far more helpful to clinicians accused of malpractice than the old, dangerously inaccurate maxim, "If you don't write anything down, they can't hang you with it."

Be cautious also when discussing the case with co-treaters, such as cotherapists or physicians who may have prescribed medication as you provided psychotherapy. Professional interchange (e.g., to prevent other tragedies or mishaps) is certainly appropriate, but your communication is almost certainly *not* protected from discovery by a plaintiff's attorney.

Support for Treatment Staff and Other Patients

Discussions with staff (and other patients, when suicide occurs on a hospital unit or involves a member of a therapy group) are often important, and may be standard parts of a routine from which any deviation would appear defensive or evasive. Avoid discussing blame, guilt, clinical details, second-guessing, and the like in such settings, and focus on the "support" aspects of the meeting. When patients ask what caused the patient's suicide, or why no one prevented it, it is often reasonable to say such things as, "It's hard to know," "Every situation is different," or "We need to respect _____'s confidentiality (and/or the family's privacy)"; then turn the group's attention to ways of dealing with patient or staff feelings and ward or group issues.

Avoid Any Appearance of Dishonesty

NEVER alter or remove any records. Larger organizations may have a policy of sealing the record after significant incidents and suicides. If there is a staff meeting, don't make it one at which staff members might appear to be "getting their stories straight."

If there is an indication of legal action, or even of dissatisfaction with your care, notify your insurance carrier. Your malpractice insurance representative should be called if someone asks for your records, a lawyer contacts you, and so on; if you are an employee of an organization, refer such requests to a senior supervisor. DO NOT discuss the case in any way without guidance from either the carrier or an attorney.

Releasing Records

DO NOT give original patient records to anyone who doesn't have very official permission to take them (such as a search warrant that includes removing records). Certain kinds of subpoenas or search warrants may entitle a law enforcement officer or court to collect original materials as evidence, but this is very unlikely in civil litigation. If you provide copies, with appropriate authorization, the person to whom you release copies may be entitled to verify that the entire record is properly copied; consider having a witness to the copying or sending the records to a professional legal copy service (seek instructions from the carrier or your lawyer). DO NOT allow the patient's family or lawyer to do the copying or to take any records out of your office without specific guidance from your attorney.

Be certain that the person who requests the records is entitled to them before releasing any information; he or she may need a subpoena, or the privilege may not clearly pass to the heirs. You don't want to appear defensive or evasive; just quietly contact your lawyer or carrier for guidance. Even simple release of the records may have legal implications, and may require special procedures; *don't assume that you know what to do.*

WHEN THERE IS DANGER TO OTHERS

S INCE THE *Tarasoff* decision, no topic has raised more discussion and
controversy among therapists than the so-called "duty to warn."

Many years ago, in a faraway land the natives call California, there arose a
therapeutic situation that was to be linked to personal tragedy and legal precedent. We call this saga *Tarasoff vs. The Regents of The University of
California.*[24]

A Mr. Podar was seeing a psychotherapist at the University of California.
He had a superficial relationship with a woman named Tatiana Tarasoff, but
believed, perhaps as a result of paranoia and/or his East Indian background,
that she was romantically committed to him. After she declined his affections, he told his therapist he was going to kill her. Ms. Tarasoff was out of
the country at that time.

The therapist believed he was serious, and sent a note to the campus
police warning of the danger and suggesting that they intervene. His supervisors quickly learned of the note and, believing such a warning was a
violation of the clinician's obligation of confidentiality, they retrieved the note

---

[24] Please do not think that I am making light of the pain endured by Tatiana Tarasoff
and her family. The fact is, the *Tarasoff* case took place decades ago and the story has
reached mythical proportions.

WHEN THERE IS DANGER TO OTHERS

and asked the police to ignore the warning. Soon after Ms. Tarasoff returned, Podar killed her.

The Tarasoff family sued the university. The therapist was released from the suit (or found not to be responsible), since he had tried to protect Tatiana. The supervisors, however, and by association their university employers, were found liable for not warning Tatiana when the therapist believed there was a substantial chance of serious injury. The case was appealed to the California Supreme Court, where the American Psychiatric Association filed an *amicus* brief in support of the defendant university. The APA's position was that protecting the sanctity of therapist–patient privilege was more important than a single, arguably unpredictable and unavoidable tragedy, and that to uphold such a breach of privilege would irreparably damage the ability of patients such as Podar to get appropriate treatment. The California Supreme Court didn't buy it, and found a duty to warn, later reestablished as a duty to *protect*, certain third parties, in California.

Make no mistake: Clinicians are not, should not be, and are not qualified to be general protectors of the public safety. That is the job of law enforcement professionals and legislators. This chapter discusses certain legal and ethical duties that arise from the special relationship between clinician and patient; it does not take the position that therapists have any special ability to predict violence, prevent it once it is imminent, or change the minds of people who insist on carrying it out. People who are generically "dangerous" should not be referred to mental health professionals to be made less dangerous unless a qualified clinician believes that the danger arises from a mental illness that can reasonably be treated using available resources, *and that the danger can be contained while treatment proceeds*. At other times, call the cops, not the shrinks.

WHAT DANGEROUSNESS ASSESSMENT DOES THE STANDARD OF CARE REQUIRE?

If there is no reason to suspect danger to others, and the patient has come to you for something unrelated to suspicion of danger to others, you probably have no duty to carry out any formal dangerousness assessment. A patient with simple phobia, for example, seeking psychotherapy or desensitization, need not endure the taking of a comprehensive history, a physical exam, and psychiatric evaluation. In some psychodynamic psychotherapy, including psychoanalysis, much of the history is gathered fairly informally, over several sessions, with no special dangerousness assessment.

Patients suspected of serious character pathology or certain Axis I disorders (e.g., psychotic, substantial impulse control, or severe mood disorders) should receive a more thorough assessment, including attention to danger to self or others. Since inpatient care today often implies some danger per se, admission workups and discharge planning should routinely consider it. Hospital and large clinic procedures often use some form of checklist or standardized protocol for this purpose. These are best used as screening devices and prompts to consider clinical and safety issues, not as ends in themselves.

Once a screening format has revealed some potential danger, it is the clinician's (usually the attending physician's) responsibility to read the note and act on it as appropriate. This does not mean that the standard always requires a complete dangerousness workup, either on admission or discharge, but attention should be paid to initial screening, and suggestions of dangerousness at admission or during hospitalization should be addressed prior to discharge (e.g., in the treatment and/or discharge plan).

When there is reason to suspect danger to others, some assessment or consideration should be made (and documented) whenever the patient's access to reasonably inferred victims increases. Moving from a locked unit to an open one, for example, offers more opportunity for elopement and potential danger to the community. The first unaccompanied pass off the ward is another time to assess, and document, safety issues. Off-grounds passes are a third step in the hierarchy, this time with the assumption that the patient will have access to people and settings that may be associated with stresses and potential dangers not easily estimated in the comparatively artificial hospital environment.

Can we really predict danger to others? Wrong question. There are a number of good, recent studies and papers on the subject. However, the point of this chapter is that you may be *expected* to "predict" danger if a jury believes it was reasonable for you to do so. The following sections assume that you reasonably should have recognized some danger, and discuss what should be done after that recognition.

DUTY TO WARN OR PROTECT

Clinicians often misunderstand the law about their duty, if any, to warn or protect others from their patients. As for most other areas of potential liability, I encourage therapists not to assume that they know what is legally required or expected, but to refer to specific statutes, reliable professional guidelines, and attorney guidance. On the other hand, you know more about patient care than do lawyers, and should be cautious about accepting quasi-clinical advice from nonclinicians.

Duty to warn or protect is a state-by-state matter. One state's laws and/or lawsuit precedents do not affect another's. More important, a duty may exist *before* a court confirms it. Most states that have had a rational lawsuit alleging a duty to warn or protect have established some precedent for plaintiffs. Thus clinicians in states that have no specific law or legal precedent to clarify the matter should still assume that there is such a duty, and should act accordingly to avoid becoming "test cases" for their jurisdictions.

WHEN DOES THE DUTY BEGIN?

Generally speaking, the duty to warn or protect arises when (1) a special relationship is present (e.g., that of therapist–patient) *and* (2) the clinician has (or should have) reason to suspect real danger to others. In some states, the law or case law doesn't recognize a duty until a specific person or class of potential victims is apparent; in others, any danger is sufficient. I suggest, without purporting to give legal advice, that therapists who have reason to suspect real danger to life or limb take whatever action is feasible to decrease the danger (see below).

Of course, different clinicians have different thresholds for "reason to suspect real danger." Be aware of warning signs, and if they appear, document the things that lead you to act, either to protect or not. You are responsible for knowing the warning signs. If a tragedy occurs, the injured person or a family member may allege that it was *foreseeable*. The question is often not whether or not you were aware of significant danger, but whether or not a person in your profession and situation is reasonably expected to be aware of it. As in other allegations of negligence, it is easy to draw conclusions after one knows the outcome, and more difficult to recreate the circumstances under which the clinician had to assess the patient and consider action.

Duty without danger? When there is no reasonably apparent danger, there can be no duty to warn or protect. Similarly, any duty to "warn" may be greatly decreased if the potential victim already knows of the danger (assuming it is the same general danger as that reasonably apparent to the therapist). Nevertheless, plaintiffs sometimes try to convince juries that a tragedy alone creates the duty.

> A man referred for hospital admission had threatened to kill himself and made some vague comments about anger at his wife, who had left him and, unknown to the doctor, feared him, had obtained a restraining order, and was hiding from him at a friend's home. She did not know he was being considered for admission, and probably thought he was still in the community. The man was not admitted, and within a short time, he found his wife, and then killed her and himself. The doctor was sued for, among other things, not warning the wife.
>
> A jury found that he had no duty to warn her since (1) there was no clear indication that the doctor could have known of her being in serious danger (not merely the object of some vague anger), (2) he didn't know where she was, and (3) her behavior suggested that she already felt a severe danger and was protecting herself, without any warning from the doctor.

Are clinicians good arbiters of what dangers are "real" or "serious"? It seems unfair to ask us to make judgments that are often well outside our expertise (such as whether or not a person's expression of anger places someone else in no, mild, or severe danger, or whether or not a delusional patient will be one of the few who commit a violent act in the near future). Nevertheless, we are expected to do our best, and some of us routinely participate in commitment and detention decisions. When in doubt, call a colleague for a consultation.

WHO IS THE POTENTIAL VICTIM?

The identity of the victim(s) has some practical importance, and in some states affects your legal responsibility to warn or protect. The simplest case is a threat, virtually any threat, against the President of the United States. You must, by law, notify the U.S. Secret Service, regardless of concerns about confidentiality, and regardless of whether or not you think the threat is genuine.[25] The Secret Service does a good job, and very rarely causes problems for the patient.

In some states, your duty applies only to *specific, named victims,* such as a spouse or a group of coworkers. In others, the therapist is required to take steps to protect a *larger, vague group* (such as all children from a child molester or all potential passengers from a suicidal bus driver). Sometimes danger alone is sufficient, with *no victim class,* and the clinician is expected to act to protect anyone believed to be in substantial danger from the patient (e.g., anyone in the community from a psychotic patient who sets fires). State requirements can change, of course. States whose early precedent-setting cases refer to a specific victim may have later ones that expand the duty to a larger group.

DISCHARGING THE DUTY

There are several ways to warn or protect potential victims. Prudent clinicians try to balance the therapeutic interests of the patient, the obligation of confidentiality, and the need to protect others from real danger. When dangerousness becomes a serious issue, it must outweigh the other two considerations. Therapeutic interests are not served by allowing a patient to hurt someone else when it reasonably can be prevented, or even by spending valuable therapeutic energy worrying about whether or not someone might be hurt between sessions.

---

[25] As a practical matter, I'm sure many patients who mention the President are not reported; nevertheless, the duty exists. The Secret Service is not as secret as most people think; its telephone number can be found in the U.S. Government listings of any city phone book.

Similarly, as we have already discussed (Chapter 9), patient privacy is far from absolute, and intact confidentiality is cold comfort when someone has been killed, seriously injured, or terrorized.

"Discharging the duty" refers to carrying out *legal* (not necessarily ethical or physically protective) requirements. If you have "discharged" some duty to warn or protect, you have fulfilled it in the eyes of the law. This is not quite the same as saying that you have "done all you can," or met clinical or ethical guidelines (Chapter 2). The requirements for discharge of the duty vary from state to state, are often poorly defined, and may not be defined at all in your state. Note also that some methods are not appropriate in some situations. For example, the police may be able to pass along a warning to a potential victim, but probably cannot arrest a patient before he or she commits a crime (serious threats, however, are often a crime). All of your reporting or warning must be done in good faith, with a reasonable expectation of substantial danger (sometimes defined in state law), and both the action and your decision-making process should be scrupulously documented.

Here are some actions that *may* discharge your duty in your state. Remember, it may be that none of the following is appropriate, feasible, or sufficient to discharge your duty completely and eliminate liability, unless your state has a statute saying that it does.

- **Call the police.** Many states specifically allow a therapist to notify a law enforcement agency of substantial danger from a patient and confirm that this is not a breach of privilege. One is generally entitled to rely on the police to take appropriate action, and this may be all that is necessary to protect you from liability. Sometimes, of course, the police take no action; their version of "protection" may be, for many reasons, different from yours.
- **Call the potential victim.** This sounds simple, but often the potential victim is not available, or the patient may not disclose his or her identity. If you do make contact, you are likely to hear two things: "What should I do?" and "Why can't you keep him in custody?" I suggest that clinicians refrain from recommendations about how to protect oneself. It is outside our experience and expertise, and there are people who are much better at it than we are (e.g., the police). One may wish to provide contact

information about battered women's shelters or (e.g., child) protection agencies, but refrain from giving legal or law enforcement advice. With regard to the second question, be cautious about giving privileged information; you are warning, not discussing the patient personally. If asked, for example, why the patient can't be held in the hospital, a comment such as "That's not possible right now" seems better than "He's not committable," particularly if the potential victim does not already know the psychiatric history. If the contact is made because the patient has left the hospital or clinic against advice (e.g., eloped from an inpatient unit), this should be communicated, as well as some estimate of when the patient left.

- **Have the patient participate in communication with the potential victim.** This increases patient participation, may increase potential responsibility, helps define the reality of the situation, and can be therapeutic.
- **Get qualified consultation.** It is not a breach of privilege to talk with a clinical colleague about your patient, as long as it is a legitimate consultation in the patient's interest (and avoiding violence is, in my opinion, virtually always in his or her interest).
- **Share decision-making responsibility** among, for example, team members. This is similar to consultation, but adds a decision-making component in which team members discuss their views of the patient and agree on matters of safety regarding such things as inpatient privileges, passes, or discharge. The agreement need not be unanimous, but evidence of careful consideration should be documented. Physicians know that they generally are responsible for medical decisions, but evidence of a team process is helpful.
- **Treat the patient.** Many forms of danger can be reduced or eliminated, temporarily or permanently, with proper diagnosis and treatment. If treatment can proceed without endangering a potential victim, this should be a primary consideration. In many cases, inpatient care is prudent. The patient, of course, must cooperate with treatment; if he or she declines, consider civil commitment.
- **Take steps to have the patient committed or detained for**

treatment. "Take steps" reminds us that clinicians themselves don't detain or commit. Rather, we recommend detention to others (such as law enforcement officers or judges) who are authorized to curtail the patient's liberty and place him or her in a treatment environment. Such a recommendation shifts a great deal of the protective burden to the law enforcement system, judge, or other decision-making official, but the process should not be entered into lightly. Some situations raise a so-called "duty to commit," in which the standard of care requires careful consideration of involuntary treatment. As mentioned earlier, commitment requires both a mental illness and some form of danger to self (through suicide or deterioration) or others. One alone is not enough.

- **Follow organization/hospital policies and procedures.** They do not necessarily define the standard of care, but they are likely to have been created in consultation with an attorney (as well as qualified clinicians), to compare favorably with the policies and procedures of similar organizations, and to offer above-the-standard guidance.

- **Involve a lawyer in your decision** (see below). Large clinics, hospitals, and professional organizations have attorneys who are available to address just this kind of question. Do not expect—or allow—the lawyer to usurp the clinician's role, however; use him or her to deal with the legal question.

Simply talking with the patient about the potential danger, or eliciting a promise or "contract" that he or she will not harm someone, may be part of the overall therapeutic process, but it is unlikely to discharge any duty to protect if the problem is substantial. Don't rely on it.

Finally, the concept of duty to warn or protect includes those conditions that clinicians are required by statute to report (e.g., child or other abuse, illness that significantly interferes with safe driving or piloting, serious criminal plans, contagious disease, and disease-spreading behavior). In most states, the duty is discharged by reporting to an appropriate law enforcement, child protective, or regulatory agency in some specified way. Some legally required reporting may not be obvious, especially to nonmedical clinicians; find out about the laws in your state.

Is the Potential Victim in Danger Right Now?

Clinicians often assume that if the patient is in the hospital when the threats are made, there is no real danger since no potential victim is available to the patient. This may discourage warning or notifying the police, with the idea that the situation will be reassessed later. While I agree with this general premise, there are several caveats to consider.

First, the victim doesn't become available merely at discharge. He or she is reachable by the patient the first time the patient leaves the psychiatric unit unescorted. Thus the first off-unit privileges or off-grounds pass for a potentially dangerous patient should be an occasion to assess danger to others carefully. Be sure a reasonable decision process is followed. This may be the time to call an identified potential victim, even though you will have to deal with the inevitable question, "If you think I might be in danger, why the heck are you letting him out?"

What Do You Tell the Patient About Warning/Protecting Potential Victims?

I suggest talking with the patient about notification or other protective action. It becomes a point for reality testing and for understanding the consequences of his or her actions. I do *not* recommend allowing the patient to "talk you out of" notification. This is a matter of legal and ethical duty in which you have already decided that there is a significant danger to another person; it is not a situation in which you, however figuratively, collude with the patient or subtly teach him or her to keep certain thoughts private.[26] In the best case, particularly in domestic situations, you and the patient may contact the potential victim together (with you listening on the extension). One should not, however, physically

---

[26] This concept is similar to that with some suicidal patients in which the clinician has thoughtfully concluded that the patient is a serious danger to himself or herself and that some protective action, such as involuntary hospitalization, must be taken. At that point, it is almost always a mistake to change one's mind just because the patient (or family, in many cases) says that he or she didn't mean it.

intrude into the middle of a domestic or other dangerous situation. Having a spouse come in for a conjoint session is one thing; going to the home when there is a threat of violence is quite another (even the police hate doing that).

The thought that warning or protecting a potential victim will seriously damage the therapeutic relationship with the potential "perpetrator" has been greatly exaggerated by opponents of any "duty to warn." Therapists raise several issues in this area, but none tips the balance toward allowing substantial danger to go unheralded. The issues include possible loss of the patient's trust, overreacting to a sensational statement (the threat) when it is not really the main therapeutic issue, being seduced into surrogate acting out on the patient's behalf (e.g., scaring the potential victim for the patient), being sued for breach of privilege, damaging the therapeutic relationship when there may not be a significant danger, unnecessarily damaging the patient (or his or her reputation), and fear of retaliation by the patient.

The above issues sometimes have their roots in clinicians' fears for their own safety, and not primarily in therapeutic considerations. When I talk with therapists or trainees about danger to others, they inevitably say something like, "How can I tell him I'm going to warn his wife when he's already mad, bigger than me, might have a weapon, and I'm the only person between him and the victim?" Good question, and not one that can always be answered. The point is that you have a duty to do whatever is feasible to protect the potential victim. You don't have a duty, so far as I know, to put yourself in danger in the process, but there's usually some way to try to help.

WHAT ABOUT FEDERAL PRIVACY LAWS REGARDING SUBSTANCE-ABUSE PATIENTS?[27]

Given the same concerns about danger, I do not differentiate between patients with and without substance-abuse diagnoses, or between those in substance-abuse programs and in other settings. It certainly doesn't

[27] As in the rest of this book, these comments should not be construed as legal advice.

matter to the potential victim. It seems reasonable to me to avoid mentioning anything about substance abuse or a substance-abuse facility to the potential victim, provided you believe that omitting such information is not relevant to his or her safety. Once again, think first about safety; no one is served if a tragedy occurs.

HELP FROM LAWYERS AND PROFESSIONAL ORGANIZATIONS

In addition to clinical consultation (Gutheil's "never worry alone"), one good-faith act that goes a long way toward protecting the clinician from liability is consultation with either an attorney experienced in clinical reporting matters or your professional organization. Local organizations may not be sophisticated enough to offer reliable advice, but state and national ones have probably wrestled with your type of dilemma many times.

A man was referred to a psychiatrist and a psychologist by his lawyer because of depression and frustration after losing a very large lawsuit award. After he became their patient, he told both that he was planning to kill the judge and all the lawyers. Both clinicians were convinced that he was serious, since he described stalking the judge, hiding a fake bomb on his lawyer's car ("to see how I could do it"), and other ominous acts committed in a cold, vengeful manner. The clinicians talked about warning or protective actions and agreed that he was very dangerous. Both had discussed the fantasies and actions with the patient in the clinical settings and decided that treatment alone was unlikely to make him less dangerous within the near future; the threats appeared to arise from a psychopathic character, not depression or psychosis. He was not commitable. State statute and case law gave no guidance; at the time, no permission-to-warn precedent had been set in that state's courts.

The clinicians contacted the patient's lawyer (who knew the patient was in treatment) for guidance, thinking that he would be frightened by the threats against him. The lawyer refused to do anything and warned the doctors about breach of privilege. They then consulted with experienced colleagues, all of whom agreed that the danger was great and that some form of warning not only was appropriate but was necessary. Finally, they contacted attorneys for their professional organizations (the American Psychological Association and American Psychiatric Association), who advised that reporting or warning was necessary and ethical.

The clinicians notified the judge, who quickly had the patient arrested for threatening a court official. He was sent to a federal prison hospital for evaluation, where he remained for several months. Upon release, he sued both clinicians for breach of privilege, lost at the trial level, appealed, and eventually lost in the state supreme court. The good-faith efforts of the clinicians to find out how to proceed properly (largely by talking with the various lawyers), while taking the danger to others very seriously, were persuasive in their defense.

· 12

DEALING WITH IMPAIRED
OR UNETHICAL COLLEAGUES

E VERY MAJOR ORGANIZATION of mental health professionals has ethical guidelines that require members to take steps to protect patients
from impaired or unethical colleagues. Those concepts can become
legal issues in at least two ways: (1) by establishing a civil professional standard by which reasonable clinicians are expected to protect
patients from known dangers of certain impaired or unethical colleagues and (2) through statutes or administrative rules governing one's
professional license. Good-faith reporting of known, or reasonably suspected, problems that may affect patient care or safety is necessary, and
should never be construed as unfair or "disloyal" to one's peer.

Unlike professional associations, licensing boards[28] have rules and
actions that carry the force of law. Many require their licensees to
report not only when they are *certain* about colleagues' specified conditions or behaviors, but also when they have reasonable *suspicions*.
This may sound heavy-handed at times (and hard to define), but one
should remember that clinical practice is a privilege, not a right. States
regulate it and are generally entitled, within boundaries, to dictate your

---

[28] In this chapter, "licensing board" refers to the state agency that provides your license
or certifies your ability to practice (and generally regulates your profession). It may be
called something else, such as a "board of healing arts" or a "board of professional
practices."

duty in both practice and reporting. If you fail to report unsafe, incompetent, or illegally acting colleagues as required, you can easily hurt both patients and your profession, and become vulnerable to liability and licensure sanctions yourself.

Many ethical violations are represented in statutes and regulations, but ethical violations per se are not matters of law unless some government body or agency has made them so; professional and organizational ethics are generally private, not legal, matters. Everyone is subject to laws and regulations; enforcement of ethical canons or guidelines applies only to one's status in the organization that recognizes them.

Nevertheless, being sanctioned for ethics violations has (and should have) considerable influence on juries, credentialing bodies, and employers. Many organizations' adverse actions based on ethics committee recommendations, such as censure or expulsion, are public, and are sometimes automatically communicated to other members, licensing boards, and even national data banks. In addition, protecting patients by appropriately reporting colleagues is part of the professional standard that applies to all practitioners.

What is a "reasonable" likelihood of danger to patients when considering whether or not to report a colleague? The reporting rules in your state probably use such wording as requiring clinicians to report colleagues when they "reasonably suspect that the (therapist, counselor, physician) may not be able to practice safely and competently, or when his or her behavior is such that it is likely to create a danger to patients or clients." I have no magic definition. Some states want to hear about every suspicion, and to sort them out with their own investigations. Others are much more liberal. When in doubt, call the board and ask.

What about liability for reporting itself? What if the colleague sues you? That's where "good faith" comes in. You are well protected from suit as long as you have made a reasonable effort to see that your concerns are supported and it is clear that your interest is to protect patients. If the person you report is in "competition" with you, or you might otherwise benefit personally from his or her being reported, be certain that you have documented your concerns well.

A surgeon's operating privileges were suspended because of questions regarding his competence in the operating room. He sued the staff committee that recommended the suspension for slander, libel, and restraint of trade. He alleged that the people who were the appropriate surgical professionals to assess his competency also competed with him for patients, and that they had colluded to remove him for their personal gain. The hospital called expert witnesses, who testified that, based on operative reports, medical charts, and nurses' statements, the hospital and its medical staff were correct in their concern, and were entitled, even required, to remove him from the operating room.

Do you have a duty to report a colleague's censure by his or her professional organization to, for example, an employer, clinical staff, or licensing board? Probably not, and such reporting could easily be construed as a personal attack; however, when you need to share or report your belief that there is a danger to patients, and an organization's public sanction supports your point, it is appropriate to mention it. Note that if the organization's action is public, you have a good defense (the truth), so long as you stick to the published wording.

If you discover safety, incompetence, or illegality issues in the context of your serving on a peer review or ethics committee, should you report it? Not to anyone except persons authorized to receive information from the peer review body, and within the purpose of that body. The law recognizes the fact that strict confidentiality in these settings is necessary for them to be effective. Federal and state law regulates who can receive information from them, and the few circumstances in which information (often conclusions or summaries rather than details) can be shared with specified bodies. It is very important that everyone associated with peer review and ethics committees understand the strict rules under which they operate, so that these protections are not threatened. Committee members can be, and have been, sued for divulging damaging information outside those rules.

What about reporting clinicians of a different profession, such as psychologists reporting physicians or social workers? Licensing boards usually have jurisdiction over only the people whom they license; medical boards can't tell social workers what to do. Many states have broad licensing agencies that cover more than one profession, however, and some have statutes that require professionals to report unsafe or illegal practices to whatever agency has jurisdiction over the clinician in question. Virtually all licensing agencies have some way of receiving complaints from the public; any clinician may use this vehicle to report a colleague, but whether or not there is a duty to do so is unclear.

IMPAIRED COLLEAGUES

Every licensing board has a mechanism, almost always a requirement, for reporting or otherwise protecting the public from impaired professionals. Good-faith reporting is a matter of both law and ethics; it must not be avoided. Most impairments, particularly in the medical professions, stem from substance abuse; a minority are attributable to physical or mental illness. Characterologic problems (e.g., from "personality disorders") will not be considered "mental illness" for our purposes, but relate to ethics and unscrupulous or illegal behavior.

Many states and agencies have provisions for the rehabilitation of substance-abusing professionals; some allow them to participate in treatment programs—especially peer-sponsored ones— without being reported (as long as progress is being made). Clinicians who treat professionals should be aware of relevant laws and ethical guidelines, however, since a practice that places patients or the public at risk must not continue.

Licensing boards and agencies often postpone or modify actions against licensees who report themselves or seek treatment voluntarily. In Texas, for example, physician substance abusers who report themselves to the Board of Medical Examiners are almost always offered confidential treatment and supervision without a public Board action. Those who are reported by someone else (or who do not accept the conditions of treatment and monitoring) are dealt with harshly (and often publically). Even a few hours can make a difference; if you know that you are going to be reported and don't make it to the Board first, you're out of luck.

Physical illness, including dementia and the fallibility of advanced age, have less stigma but are just as important to recognize and report. In such situations, one usually meets with less resistance when recommending that a colleague voluntarily report himself or herself to the Board and suspend or curtail practice, but it is difficult nonetheless.

One should not accept a colleague's promise to report himself or herself or to change his or her behavior. Such promises are simply not reliable enough to risk patient injury (and your liability), and sometimes the colleague's own life and health. Similarly, secretly treating a fellow clinician with a patient-threatening condition may seem the humane thing to do, but is often a real mistake.

An alcohol-abusing clinician was confronted by his colleagues on the professional staff of a mental health clinic. They strongly recommended that he seek treatment and mentioned that the licensing board might have some ways of helping without suspending his license. In deference to his past experience and career, however, they accepted his promise that he would "seriously look into treatment and maybe report myself . . . I sure don't want to hurt anybody." They decided not to report him and did not follow up on his promise to "look into" it.

Less than a week later, he committed suicide, while intoxicated, leaving a note that said, in effect, that he could not stand the embarrassment of losing his license and seeing his career end in humiliation. He said that he saw no way out but to end his life, and hoped that his family and colleagues would remember the good things he had done in his life. Had he been reported (or reported himself), there would have been a good chance for rehabilitation, and, if successful, he would not have "seen his career end in humiliation."

If you are treating a colleague under an order from a licensing board, must you report every detail of the clinician-patient's therapy and verbalizations, or supply copies of your notes to the licensing board? Generally not, but be certain this has been agreed upon in advance (the board's rules and expectations should have been made clear to you). If you have an opportunity to influence the reporting rules, try to be sure they are consistent with good treatment and a therapeutic environment. Board orders may require great (generally unnecessary) detail, perhaps because some board members (often lay appointees) do not understand the need for some privacy in treatment. Medical boards, for example, may not include a psychiatrist or substance-abuse professional and thus often don't understand how the psychotherapeutic approach really works. Board members from outside the profession may bring other fears and stereotypes to the process as well, but it is also true that some psychologists or other mental health clinicians on such boards may not be knowledgeable or objective enough to deal with the combination of public safety and rehabilitative issues.

A mental health professional was censured for stalking and harassing a clinic employee. The licensing board required treatment by a psychoanalytically trained therapist for not less than three years, with the therapist's notes to be available to the board upon demand. The professional asked the board to reconsider both the arbitrary duration and the complete loss of confidentiality, and convinced them that such a requirement would undermine the therapeutic effort. Indeed, she had been unable to find a psychoanalyst willing to treat her under those conditions.

Resist the temptation to subvert the treatment-reporting requirement, even subtly. Acknowledge the conflict of agency between your role of therapist and that of monitor for the board, and then try to be as honest as you can. You can suggest that the board appoint a third party to evaluate your clinician-patient from time to time. Urine drug screening, for example, is highly recommended for substance abusers, but is best done by a representative of the board or an impaired-clinician committee rather than by the treating clinician (although the results should be shared with the latter).

LETTERS OF REFERENCE OR RECOMMENDATION

Professional references are very serious documents. It is unethical and a disservice to future patients to misrepresent a colleague's qualifications or character in a letter of reference. If a person or organization accepts an unqualified clinician based on a knowingly misleading statement from you, then you bear some responsibility for any damage he or she does that an honest reference might have prevented. Dishonesty is a matter of omission as well as commission; leaving out important derogatory information is the same as lying about positive things.

A social worker accused of engaging in sex with patients was offered an opportunity to resign rather than endure termination proceedings, provided he would give up any right to contest the allegations (which were extensively supported by answering-machine recordings and other evidence). His employer, a large mental health center, agreed not to report him to the state licensing agency if he left the clinic. A few weeks later, his former supervisor received a standard request from another clinical program for a professional reference. The form asked about any unethical behavior, patient complaints, disciplinary actions, and, as is common today, "any other occurrence or condition that might interfere with safe and competent clinical practice."

The former supervisor asked for guidance from his employer's human resources department, and was told that he must not say anything about the social worker's problems, apparently because of the latter's resignation agreement. He chose to complete the form with bland statements, neither very complimentary nor mentioning the sexual impropriety.[29]

Over a year later, one of the social worker's patients at the new clinic committed suicide, and in the suicide note cited an affair with him during which she had become pregnant. The social worker and clinic were sued. At deposition, the social worker admitted having sex with patients at the old clinic, and that the old clinic had allowed him to resign without any investigation or reporting. The plaintiff, armed with the new information, added both the old clinic and the supervisor to the suit. The clinic sought dismissal for itself, saying that the responsibility to notify the new clinic was the supervisor's, since it was he who had received the reference request, and that his response was not a part of his employment with them. The court found that the clinic's personnel reference policy was within the administrative standard, but the supervisor's knowing omission of important information was below his professional standard. Nevertheless, the clinic shared the financial responsibility because providing an honest reference for a former clinical employee was considered to be within routine professional duties.

Organizations often have policies against detailed letters of reference or recommendation. They, or their lawyers, believe they can avoid legal problems by limiting all such communications to some

---

[29] What would have happened if he had declined to provide a reference is not clear in this case. Some employers would consider that a "signal" that something was wrong; others might simply have understood the organization's policy against providing detailed information.

thing simple and sanitary, such as dates of employment and the fact that the person left in good standing. I strongly advise clinicians who agree to provide references to be honest and clear. Following organization policy is usually a good thing, but in this case, one's duty to the recipient of the reference (e.g., other employer, clinical staff, licensing board, or hospital), and through the recipient to future patients, is more important. If your signature is on the reference, you are warranting that the information is correct to the best of your knowledge. If you know that a serious problem exists, reveal it in good faith or decline to provide the reference.

· 13

ADVERSE AND SIDE EFFECTS OF TREATMENT

A NUMBER OF LAWSUITS against mental health professionals, especially psychiatrists, are associated with adverse effects of treatment. Bad effects, however, do not necessarily (or even usually) imply any deviation from the standard of care or a substandard (treatment) product. Medication adverse effects are the most common source of this kind of lawsuit, but other treatments can be implicated as well. We will not focus here on biological treatments.

I think of "side effects" as qualitatively different from "adverse effects," the latter being more serious and generally less common. Sometimes adverse effects of therapy are expected (cf., alopecia [hair loss] and severe nausea with many kinds of cancer chemotherapy). In a few cases and therapies, adversity may be necessary to the treatment's success.

From the patient's viewpoint, the concept of psychotherapy side effects includes effects of the transference; changes in marital and family relationships; feelings and behaviors that arise as unconscious material approaches consciousness, becomes available, and is worked through; responses to one's new (often positive) behaviors and coping styles; and responses of others in the environment to those new attitudes and behaviors. Patients differ in their ability to modulate their own change, and therapists (and therapeutic situations) differ in their ability to help in that effort. Many new feelings and behaviors are expected parts of the therapy process, and often indicate positive behavioral or intrapsychic changes; however, change is difficult for many patients and their families. Never underestimate people's reluctance to change, even when they say they want to.

> After several months of psychodynamically oriented therapy, a patient announced that she was going to divorce her husband. "I finally see that I married him because I was immature" . . . "I wanted the father I never really had" . . . "Now that I'm growing in therapy, I realize he's not healthy for me." In spite of suggestions that she postpone action and use the therapy to examine other possible reasons for her impulse to divorce, she met with a lawyer. The lawyer advised her to protect her interests by, among other things, withdrawing most of the money from the family bank account.
>
> When her husband discovered what he thought was unusual behavior in a previously stable marriage, she told him that therapy had shown her that the marriage was a terrible mistake, and implied that her therapist had indirectly encouraged divorce by recommending that she behave more independently. She demanded that her husband leave the home; divorce and child custody proceedings ensued.
>
> Over the next few months, the patient reconciled with her husband. During the same period, she decreased the frequency and intensity of her psychotherapy sessions. Eventually, she reported that she no longer needed a therapist; her family and church would give her the strength and rewards she needed. She declined the therapist's recommendation to explore her termination impulse (and to compare it with her impulse to divorce), and stopped treatment a week later. A few months after that, the therapist received notice of a lawsuit alleging negligent psychotherapy, with the suggestion that he had attempted to engineer the divorce as part of some misguided treatment plan. The suit was eventually dropped.

Many so-called adverse effects are not related to the treatment at all. Patients may erroneously believe that their problems are associated with a clinician's intervention for a number of reasons. Some believe that if a problem is temporally associated with the treatment, it must have been caused by it (cf., many breast-implant plaintiffs). Others misunderstand or misuse psychological or medical information (e.g., from television, magazines, the *Physicians' Desk Reference,* or the Internet). A large number assume that pain or tragedy is related to treatment because of a need to make sense of a confusing, frightening, ambiguous, or otherwise anxiety-producing situation. Anger (conscious or unconscious) at the clinician or a general wish to blame someone occurs as well, and can be coupled with displacement to blame the therapist. A few lawsuits are kindled by encouragement from lawyers, perhaps even in advertisements for clients ("If you've been in an accident, you may be entitled to big money"), and a few more are kept alive by attorneys' encouragement after the symptoms would ordinarily have dissipated.[30]

Before recommending a treatment, the clinician should be confident (1) that it is indicated for the condition for which it is used and (2) that the treatment is generally safe and effective when appropriately prescribed or implemented, *or* that the ratio of risks to benefits is favorable given the clinical situation. If the treatment meets these conditions, it is easy to defend the choice, although it still must be prescribed or applied within the standard of care (including informing the patient of significant risks if present).

Even risky or potentially damaging treatments may be indicated if the condition for which they are considered is serious and there are few alternatives. In medicine, patients routinely accept mutilation or extremely toxic medication when necessary. There are situations in mental health that justify approaches almost as extreme, such as sometimes are used with severe suicidal impulses, intractable violence, morbid depression, autism, certain addictions, or severe attachment disorders.

---

[30] Symptoms that continue only as long as the lawsuit is unresolved are not always caused by attorney encouragement. Plaintiff exaggeration or malingering is one factor; having to restate and reaffirm symptoms over and over through lengthy litigation is another. Even reasonable plaintiffs may be unable to resolve symptoms that are kept alive by internal conflict or ambiguity until a court, insurance company, government, or other authority figure says at last, "The decision is final; the debate is over." If the resolution is in favor of the plaintiff, the public affirmation and/or money often helps a genuine—not malingering—plaintiff to "let go" of the symptoms (a phenomenon sometimes called by lawyers a "green poultice": money applied wherever it hurts). Even when it is not in the plaintiff's favor, the clarity of a final legal resolution allows some to improve and get on with their lives, although others become frozen in their need to keep their symptoms out of neurotic or character defense, or simply to retain their posture of entitlement.

Consultation is a helpful way to establish the reasonableness of a dangerous or controversial treatment, and to establish that it is being provided according to the relevant standard of care. Even when the clinician knows that a treatment has a very good risk/benefit ratio, such as most applications of ECT, the possibility of misunderstanding may suggest a "defensive" consultation with a qualified colleague. One should always carefully document the decision and consent process associated with uncommon or professionally controversial treatments (as contrasted with those that are controversial for laypersons but are commonly accepted in the professional community).

The keys to meeting the standard for predicting, preventing, or controlling adverse effects, and/or mitigating their impact, are:

- *Proper recommendation.* Is there a safer choice that probably would be as effective in this case, or a more effective choice with similar risks?
- *Adequately informed consent* (not necessarily written; see Chapter 7). Remember that consent includes the patient's knowledge, competence, and voluntariness.
- *Appropriate prescribing and/or application of the treatment.*
- *Appropriate monitoring and follow-up* for early warnings of problems, and trying to ensure proper use of the treatment by the patient.

You are responsible for having the knowledge and experience to carry these out, and then for doing it.

· 14

FORENSIC TRAINING AND PRACTICE

M OST CLINICIANS DO some forensic work, even if it is only an occasional evaluation for competency, disability, or civil commitment. We will very briefly address a few common issues; a more complete discussion is not the purpose of this book.

Forensic tasks often seem clinical, but one should always be aware that the purpose and outcome are *not* clinical, but fall within the arena and rules of another environment. *Be sure you understand that purpose and that environment, at least enough to be able to follow its rules.*

TRAINING

One does not need formal forensic training to deal with most routine forensic requests. It may certainly increase the chance that you will do quality work, but attorneys and courts are more interested in your clinical expertise and your objectivity than in whether or not you can quote some legal term or principle. The important thing is that you understand that the legal arena is (and must be) different from the clinical one and that the two can conflict substantially. An ethical attorney will not purposely embarrass you (it would be bad for the case, after all), although he or she will try to use you to the client's advantage.

Do not hesitate to ask the lawyer what the legal issues are, and try to find out exactly what questions you are to address before you begin. The lawyer may slant matters toward his or her client; however, few will knowingly[31] give you bad legal or ethical advice.

The lawyer may or may not have a comprehensive understanding of the mental health issues in the case. I sometimes help attorneys understand the forensic psychiatric aspects of their strategies, being careful to stay out of the legal issues themselves, since most lawyers rarely deal with, for example, the psychiatric aspects of criminal responsibility. This does *not* mean that I take the client's side, but rather that I help to clarify the issues and options as I see them. Note that the psychiatric or psychological issues are usually only a small part of the overall case; the lawyer is the one who coordinates (and is responsible for) the "big picture."

A criminal defense attorney requested forensic consultation to try to avoid the death penalty in a capital murder case. He said that his client had committed the killings, and generally conceded that the man was guilty of murder (for the difference, see Chapter 2) because a court-retained psychiatrist had said that he had been responsible for his acts. In jail awaiting trial, the defendant appeared depressed but nonpsychotic, remembered the killings in some detail, and showed a great deal of remorse as he awaited what he believed was the punishment he deserved.

Careful review of the arrest records, police investigation, and witness reports revealed that the killer's behavior had been somewhat bizarre, quite sudden, out of character, and probably related to very significant emotional loss. Although he was able to carry out a moderately complex series of acts that he knew would lead to the deaths of several family members, including his small children, they were subtly ritualistic and psychologically symbolic, without any apparent self-serving purpose (such as revenge, monetary gain, or sadistic pleasure). If the perpetrator had been a woman, various postpartum and filicidal psychological syndromes would almost certainly have been strongly considered. Nevertheless, before talking with their own

---

[31] "Knowingly" includes a lot of things. Most attorneys don't specialize in mental health law, and even those who do rarely understand our ethical and professional issues. Don't rely on them *too* much.

forensic psychiatrist, the attorneys believed that the court psychiatrist's opinion, coupled with the magnitude of the killings, ensured a first-degree murder conviction.

If you anticipate doing very much forensic work, and want to be sure that you do it properly and ethically, I suggest consulting any of a number of books or attending a forensic practice workshop. I am most familiar with books for psychiatrists. Our office periodically provides one-day practical workshops for psychiatrists and other clinicians, and we market an audiocassette version of the workshop, with a comprehensive syllabus and example forms that, although "psychiatric," are largely applicable to other mental health disciplines.[32] Psychiatrists can also take advantage of an excellent three-day program given annually through the American Academy of Psychiatry and the Law; similar courses and workshops may be available through the American Psychological Association and other professional groups, as well as private vendors. Full-time, accredited fellowships are useful for those who wish to make forensic work a career. They are part of accredited specialty training programs, and are beyond the purview of this book.

EXPERT CONSULTANT, EXPERT WITNESS

Who is your client? The *lawyer* is usually your client. Sometimes forensic clinicians are retained by a court (or may have a contract to do court evaluations); however, most private forensic contact is from an attorney.[33] *Do not* allow yourself to be retained by a litigant; if someone calls wanting forensic help, tell him or her you'd be happy to talk with the person's lawyer, and then close the conversation.

---

[32] *Developing a Forensic Practice,* on seven audiocassettes, with syllabus, sample forms, etc., is available through the author at P.O. Box 4015, Horseshoe Bay, TX 78657, or by calling (830) 596-0062. Proceeds go to the Texas Depressive–Manic Depressive Association.

[33] Note that your work may be *ordered by* a court without changing the fact that it is *on behalf* of the lawyer who retained you (and his or her client). This does not mean that you are working for the court, but merely that the side that retained you is entitled to your services, that the other side must cooperate with you in some way, and/or that you are more likely to get paid for your trouble.

How Does the Lawyer–Expert Relationship Work? If you are retained by a lawyer for one side or the other, your professional relationship is with that lawyer (we'll ignore court contracts for the moment), and your responsibility is to do a thorough, competent, honest, objective job. You are hired by the lawyer to perform work, and you may be asked to testify about the results of your work; you are *not* hired to advocate for the lawyer's client (but you may advocate for any opinions you eventually form).

Do not guarantee that your assessment or opinions will be helpful to the lawyer who retains you. Your compensation should always be completely independent of whatever opinions you may eventually form or whatever testimony you may (or may not) eventually give, *and independent of the outcome of the case.* It is unethical for your fees or payment to be contingent on the outcome. Expect (in writing is best) to be paid regardless; that helps preserve your objectivity.

Do not accept forensic cases in which you have evaluated or treated the litigant in an ordinary clinical context. If a patient of yours (or his or her lawyer) asks you to become involved as an expert in his or her disability case, harassment lawsuit, or custody battle, I recommend that you decline. Your records, of course, may become part of the case and you may be asked to testify about your clinical work with the patient. If you do testify, it is a matter of ethics, in my opinion, that you refrain from offering any expert opinion (because your care of the patient has focused on clinical need rather than legal issues, and your duty to your patient—even if you are no longer treating him or her—creates a conflict of interest with the forensic purpose of an expert opinion).

There are many sources of additional information about forensic practice issues such as these, including forensic mental health journals, books, and Web sites. Those that sound "psychiatric" are often largely relevant to other professions as well. A list of resources is included in Appendix D.

EVALUATIONS

Evaluations are probably the most common forensic endeavor for the general clinician. Understanding their purpose and rules is, as noted, critical to the successful completion of the task. Do not confuse forensic evaluations with those done for a clinical purpose. Indeed any work done for a forensic purpose, no matter what the case or goal, should be approached from a perspective that is somewhat different from that of an ordinary clinician (but using your clinical skills and experience as your foundation).

Disability agencies, for example, do not want a "clinical" report (except for a clear-cut diagnosis, if one can be made). They want an assessment of abilities and functions, keyed to the way they categorize functional ability. Since no diagnosis is always disabling, it is not useful merely to say that the patient has some particular disorder. Some disability decisions are made on the basis of specific words or phrases, which have specific definitions for that agency or insurance company. Do not assume that your definition of "persistence" or "concentration," for example, is the same as that used by the Social Security Disability Section. Note also that disability entitlement may refer variously to the inability to continue a specific job (such as letter carrier for the Postal Service), the inability to work in a broad job area (such as to practice clinical social work in any form), or the inability to do any gainful work at all. Local employment opportunity may or may not be a criterion. Read the agency instructions or guidelines, stick to them, and be honest.

TESTIMONY

Testimony is not usually your purpose, but rather a possible, generally unusual, end point. If the lawyer believes that your testimony will be helpful to his or her case, you may be asked to testify. If not, don't take it personally. *Do not measure the quality of your work, your purpose, or even your usefulness to the attorney by whether or not you testify.* If your review or assessment finds information that seems counter to the litigant's interest, that's fine. Tell the lawyer (you need not write down your views unless asked). He or she may use the information to reassess the case, settle it wisely, negotiate a plea bargain, or drop a lawsuit that would be expensive for both sides.

Further discussion of testimony is beyond the purview of this book. Tell the truth. If the lawyer asks you to do otherwise, remember Shakespeare's advice at the end of Chapter 1.

CHILDREN AND ADOLESCENTS

I believe strongly that cases involving evaluation of, or opinions about, children and adolescents (especially early adolescents) almost always should be referred to forensic clinicians with extensive child and adolescent experience (and preferably specialty training). This applies especially to child custody issues (a highly complex and specialized field in itself); I see a lot of bad professional work in that highly volatile area, usually by clinicians who are seduced into incomplete evaluations (e.g., of only one parent, and sometimes of none of the children) by a lawyer, by a litigant, or, worse, by a patient.

Child psychology and psychiatry are not merely intuitive extensions of adult work, nor is routine knowledge of child development sufficient to provide the necessary expertise.

·15

ON BEING SUED

I CAN'T THINK OF many worse experiences. It's even bad when you're sure you're going to win, and if you don't, an insurance company will pay. As in psychotherapy, the dollar cost is not the most expensive part; time, energy, and emotion are almost always bigger costs.

This chapter will generally refer to malpractice actions. Someone comes to your door and serves you with an official-looking paper that says, "You have been sued." At that point, it's a done deal. You can't change anything clinically, and you are locked into a process that may take years. Call your lawyer and your insurance carrier.[34] Right now. And do everything they say.

In many jurisdictions, the plaintiff's attorney is required to notify you that he or she is considering a lawsuit. While scary, this is a good thing, since it gives your lawyer a chance to convince the plaintiff that a lawsuit is a bad idea. (This is your lawyer's job; *do not* try to do it

---

[34] You *are* insured, aren't you? This book takes the simplistic position that you have malpractice insurance, and that you regularly review your policy to be sure that it covers everything you do in your practice. It is interesting to talk philosophically about "going bare," but I don't recommend it at all. Therapists who believe they are adequately covered by employers or government indemnity should be certain that they have coverage that puts them, not the organization, first (see below). Therapists who believe that they practice under some form of government "immunity" should know that plaintiffs' lawyers have made a science of finding ways around immunity statutes.

yourself.) Lawyers don't want to file suits they are unlikely to win or settle to their advantage. Advance notice also gives your lawyer and insurance carrier time to organize a response. Notice letters often come with requests for communication or records. Don't ignore the letter, but *do not* accede to the requests without a lawyer's advice, no matter how innocuous they seem. *Refer all requests, orders, or other communications from the plaintiff or plaintiff's lawyer to your own lawyer or malpractice carrier.* Don't even provide the name of your malpractice carrier yourself; let your lawyer or insurance company respond for you.

I envy people who can put such matters into their lawyers' and carriers' hands and go on with their lives, secure in the knowledge that someone else will take care of it. Most of us (and perhaps a larger proportion of those whose personalities lead them to become psychotherapists in the first place) aren't made that way, however. It may help to remember that by the time a notice is received, all your clinical work has been over for months (or years). You are now in the legal arena; let the lawyers do their thing, help them, and try to refrain from second-guessing your clinical decisions, except to assist with your defense.

YOUR LAWYER

In this chapter, "your lawyer" means an attorney who is experienced in mental health malpractice matters and has a duty to represent your interests. In some situations, you will want a lawyer who is not representing any other defendant in your case. That is, his or her duty is to you alone, not to an insurance company, agency, clinic, hospital, and/or employer. Counsel for a public agency, for example, probably has no duty to any individual employee, but must always act in the interest of the agency *even if it harms an employee or other defendant.* The same principle applies to private hospitals, clinics, and insurance companies.

One exception to the "mental health malpractice experience" rule, in my view, is the hiring of an attorney to monitor an experienced litigator assigned to you by, for example, your employer or insurance carrier when the litigator has a substantial duty to some other defendant (e.g., a hospital or agency) or interested party (e.g., your insurance company, whose risks and goals in the litigation may not be the same as yours). Such a personal lawyer may well be worth a few hundred dollars of your own money and need not, in my experience, be intimately involved in the case. An occasional hour or so of review should be sufficient.

Malpractice and related negligence actions are often filed against several defendants, including clinicians, their employers, and organizations that offer care or award practice privileges (e.g., mental health centers or hospitals). Different defendants in the same case usually have differences in potential liability, proportion of responsibility, contribution to damage, and available money for a judgment or settlement. Plaintiffs (and, less often, defendants) routinely try to manipulate the relationships among defendants, sometimes to turn one against the other (e.g., by getting one to blame another, either overtly or by implication). A single doctor or therapist may be caught up in the process, and may be at a disadvantage when a large organization is trying to protect itself.

Fortunately, malpractice codefendants usually do not sabotage each other's cases. A hospital or government agency would be ill-advised to alienate its professional staff by unfairly blaming everything on one clinician. The defense lawyers usually work together and share talent and information. There are exceptions, however, and money is a strong motivator. Accusations of criminal behavior and sexual indiscretion are areas in which once the person is strongly implicated, he or she should not expect pleasant treatment from codefendants.

THE COMPLAINT OR PETITION

The "complaint" or "petition" is the legal document that summarizes the plaintiff's allegations. It is a very discouraging document. It doesn't say that you *may* have made a mistake; but that you *did,* and there were a dozen of them, they damaged the patient horribly, and you were reckless and uncaring in the process. It doesn't mention the times you answered calls in the middle of the night, the hard work you did during that last crisis, or all those other patients and families who appreciate what you've done for them. It doesn't give you any credit for trying to help your patient, but assumes that you had virtually no interest in his or her welfare. Explaining and defending your actions, and convincing the jury that you are not the worst clinician since Josef Mengele, is *your* job (through your lawyer), not the plaintiff's.

Is that fair? Well, yes. Remember that ours is an adversarial system. Assuming that the plaintiff believes he or she has been wronged, he or she is entitled (within reason and certain rules) to vigorous pursuit of the claim. It is unreasonable to expect the other side not to come out swinging, just as it would be unreasonable (and a breach of legal duty) for *your* lawyer to ease up on your defense. You can usually expect the plaintiff's lawyer to treat you civilly in person (such as at deposition or trial), but that's sometimes done to make you feel comfortable enough to let down your guard. Don't take it personally.

NOTIFY YOUR INSURANCE CARRIER

Your malpractice policy recommends, perhaps requires, that you notify the carrier as soon as you have reason to believe that a lawsuit might be filed. That includes not only the receipt of "notice" letters, but untoward deaths, other adverse events, and serious complaints. It is important that you follow that recommendation, and your local agent can often provide good advice. Routine notification should not prejudice your coverage or rates.

BE HONEST

The importance of not altering or hiding patient records was discussed in Chapter 1.

HELP YOUR ATTORNEY

Your lawyer is likely to ask you to do some of the spadework for your case, such as reviewing the literature and researching your records. Following the lawyer's suggestions comes under this heading as well. Although you will be asked to help him or her understand the clinical situation, clinical knowledge alone is not the point of this exercise. Communicate well (and demand the same of your lawyer); satisfy yourself that your interests are being protected, but don't be a prima donna. If you believe that you are being inadequately represented, take appropriate action; beyond that, don't try to run the show.

What If the Plaintiff Is Still Your Patient?

Do not continue to treat a person who is suing you, or has officially threatened suit (e.g., with a notice letter from an attorney). Take appropriate steps to avoid abandoning the patient, and talk with your lawyer or carrier about how such actions may affect the case. Occasionally, a plaintiff doesn't understand exactly whom he or she is suing (and in large or class-action suits, may not even know that he or she is a plaintiff). In such cases, politely break the news and terminate care in some reasonable fashion.

> A child psychiatrist was one of many clinicians sued as part of a large multiplaintiff action against dozens of doctors, therapists, and hospitals. One child's mother was unaware that she and her daughter were suing the psychiatrist until she called to make an appointment for the child, saying, "You're the only doctor who ever really helped her." He declined, and his attorney made a note of the compliment.

If a non-plaintiff patient verbally complains or threatens to sue, assess the situation (e.g., Is the patient psychotic? Angry about a specific therapy issue?) and decide whether or not continuing treatment may be imprudent for either of you. Don't assume that you must keep treating the patient for his or her well-being; therapists are rarely so critical and unique that they must tolerate personal threats.

Except as absolutely necessary to secure needed care for a plaintiff who is still your patient, don't make any statement about the case, no matter how much you think it may help, to anyone except your lawyer, your insurance carrier, your own therapist, and maybe your spouse. This caveat applies to training and employment supervisors as well. Don't contact the plaintiff or anyone associated with the plaintiff. Don't discuss the clinical case, even informally, with any other defendant or person associated with the patient's care unless your lawyer says it's O.K.

INTERROGATORIES

Interrogatories are formal questions from one side of the lawsuit to another that must be answered, or any lack of answer explained. The plaintiff will send interrogatories through your lawyer, who will need your help in answering them. Expect questions about the case, but also about such things as your insurance, finances, education, practice, past problems, and other topics. Your lawyer will advise you about questions that need not be answered for some reason (such as those that are overly onerous: "List every textbook and article from which you learned to treat patients such as the plaintiff"), and will help you to deal with the others.

EXPERT WITNESSES OR CONSULTANTS

Expert witnesses or consultants may be retained by both sides to review the facts and provide opinions. The defense experts will first help your attorney assess the merits of the case and decide upon a strategy. You should understand that a good expert works for your attorney, not for you, and will be both objective and experienced in the clinical and forensic aspects of cases such as yours. He or she thus may not come to an opinion that supports you. Your attorney will use the expert's findings to assess the strengths and weaknesses of your case, plan litigation strategy, and perhaps assist in settlement negotiations.

DEPOSITIONS

Depositions ("discovery depositions") are opportunities for each side to discover the strengths and weaknesses of the other's case. The civil system is designed to prevent those Perry Mason surprises at the last minute. Unless your case is dismissed or settled at an early stage, the plaintiff's lawyer will have an opportunity to ask you questions, under oath and in a setting as binding as a court, about almost anything related to the case except matters of lawyer–client privilege.

SETTLEMENT

By the time evidence has been exchanged, experts have rendered their reports, and witnesses for both sides have been deposed, the two sides know a great deal about each other's case. There may be good reason to avoid a trial, which is expensive and brings with it a chance of losing. A settlement may be negotiated at any time after the suit is filed, even during the trial itself.

Settlement is a dirty word to many malpractice defendants, but the fact is that most cases never go to trial. Settlement is not an admission of fault, but an acceptance of the chance that a jury (or, less commonly, a judge) will decide against you. Your malpractice policy specifies the extent of your right to refuse settlement, and many clinicians feel very strongly about having their day in court. Some policies give one the right to insist on a trial but limit the carrier's liability to the amount for which the case could have been settled. Read your policy carefully.

TRIALS

Throughout your case, your lawyer will assume that it will go to trial. He or she cannot afford to think otherwise, and neither should you.

It may take years for the case to come to trial. Once it does, the lawyer's demeanor changes dramatically. Everything comes down to a few days of extremely intense effort and rapid decisions about what parts of the now-massive case will be placed before the trier (jury and/or judge) in the limited time allowed. Between the lawyer's decisions and objections and the judge's rulings, much of what you think is important may never be aired in court. Feel free to suggest that certain points be brought out or questions asked, but trust your lawyer to decide how best to present the case.

APPEALS

The losing party may appeal the trial verdict to an appropriate higher court. Appeals courts review only matters of law (e.g., the "technicalities" of the trial process). The jury's or judge's decision of "fact" cannot be appealed (see Chapter 2).

APPENDIX A

RESULTS OF THE 1997–1998 REID/ZEIG, TUCKER NATIONAL SURVEY ON FORENSIC ISSUES IN THE MENTAL HEALTH PROFESSIONS

Respondents were selected randomly from professional organization mailing lists, with some attention to state and regional representation.

Respondents' Professional Degree	Ph.D. or other doctorate	60%
	M.S.W.	28%
	Other (master's)	12%
Respondent Gender	Female	61%
	Male	39%
Mean Years in Clinical Practice	18 (range 2–40 years)	
Clinical Group/Solo Practice	Solo practice	61%
	Same-discipline group	7%
	Multidisciplinary group	32%
Of Those in Groups:	Practice with 2–3 other clinicians	32%
	Practice with 4–10 clinicians	45%
	Practice with >10 clinicians	23%
Practice Community	Urban	45%

Suburban	42%
Rural/small town	13%

Reimbursement Method	Salaried	9%

The remainder had varying proportions of private-pay and contract practices. The response format could not determine which practices were primarily fee-for-service, managed-care contract, etc.

Primary Payment Source	HMO	17%
	Other MCO	31%
	Non-MCO	52%

Patient Load	Primarily outpatient	93%
	Primarily inpatient	0
	Mixed	7%

Primary Practice Sector	Private	87%
	Public	11%
	Academic	2%

The survey asked respondents to rank at least three legal/forensic or ethical issues that they believed were most important to **their clinical profession**, and similarly to rank at least three items most important to **their own clinical practices**.

In order to avoid prejudicing the results, this part of the survey was open-ended, with no checklists or suggestions. Some responses were quite discrete (e.g., "confidentiality" and "unethical colleagues"). Others listed subgroups of an answer already given (e.g., "confidentiality" and "managed-care confidentiality"). Some answers were very specific ("being subpoenaed in child custody cases"); others more vague ("standard of care," "managed care").

We tried to analyze the results in a way that would suggest the most common areas of concern, since we wanted to make this book relevant to practicing counselors and therapists. Nevertheless, the responses could have been "scored" in several different ways. Here is a list of the most frequent topics reported, followed by a brief discussion.

ISSUES IMPORTANT TO THE
RESPONDENT'S CLINICAL PROFESSION

	Percent listing it among the top three or four issues
Confidentiality (especially managed care; some computer/faxes)	58%
Managed care (especially adequacy of care, restraints on good care; some conflict of interest)	51%
Forensic topics (especially child custody exams and procedures; some competence)	42%
Dual relationships (conflict of interest, role clarity, bureaucracy, assess versus treat)	23%
Standard of care (including adequate training and supervision)	21%
Sexual abuse (child, other, including reporting; not sex with patients)	18%
Sex with patients (including reporting)	12%
Boundary issues other than sex (including business with patients)	12%
Colleagues' poor treatment/ethics	12%
Records/record keeping (overlaps greatly with confidentiality, managed care, etc.)	11%

Other issues, reported by at least 1% of respondents and listed in order of the number reporting, included "duty to warn," difficulty training therapists in current clinical environments, patient abuse, supervision, continuing education, litigious or lawsuit-threatening patients, therapist safety, therapists being cheated by patients, "alternative" therapies, impaired clinicians, patients getting divorced, patient rights, parental consent, child custody battles, staying within one's competence, "false memory" allegations, domestic violence, assisted suicide, HIV counseling and patient sexual activity, "do no harm," licensing requirements, monitoring/compliance and psychotropic medication, patients' lack of legal knowledge, special education law/issues. and insurance issues (unrelated to managed care).

ISSUES IMPORTANT TO THE RESPONDENT'S OWN PRACTICE

	Percent listing it among the top three or four issues
Confidentiality (especially managed care, couple/family therapy, records, test data)	58%
Managed care (especially constraints on good care, MCO forcing care, liability for MCO decision	33%
Forensic topics (especially custody evaluations; also competence, testifying)	28%
Professional competence (including maintaining competence/standards, impairment, poor training)	14%
Litigious patients	11%
Boundary issues (including sex with patients)	11%
Dual relationships	9%
Informed consent (including patient decision making)	9%
Third-party control over care (not managed care or insurance)	9%
Insurance (not managed care)	9%
General liability issues	7%
"Duty to warn"	7%
Patient rights	7%
Sexual abuse (reporting, management, confrontation)	6%

Other issues, reported by at least 1% of respondents and listed in order of the number reporting, included "alternative" therapies, child abuse, therapeutic touch (avoiding ethical problems), special education, blaming patients for failure to improve, technology, patient dishonesty, patient demands, employee malpractice (*respondeat superior* issues), patients on parole/probation (difficulty providing recommended treatment, patient dissatisfaction), parents' versus children's rights, poorly trained/misunderstanding licensing boards, psychotropic medications (recognizing poor prescribing/monitoring, overuse, noncompliance), patients' misunderstanding their legal situations, and therapist safety.

There were some surprises. The past decade has seen a notable decrease in the relative importance of suicide and duty-to-warn–like issues, and a great rise (no surprise) in issues related to managed care. Confidentiality was the largest single concern, but although over half of the respondents cited managed-care organizations (MCOs), very few mentioned the very significant threats to patient privacy posed by governments and large information systems (arguably to support health-care information needs, but of marked concern to the American Psychological Association and the American Psychiatric Association). Boundary issues and violations made a healthy showing, but were a little less of a concern than expected. There were few differences between respondents' concerns for their professions and those for their personal practices, but managed care was one topic on which there was a substantial split. Over half of the responding therapists and counselors believe managed care has detrimental legal and ethical effects, but only about a third had felt them firsthand. Similarly, many (23%) felt that dual relationships (conflict of interest and agency issues) were a serious problem for the profession; far fewer (9%) listed them as a top concern for their own practices.

The largest response categories—confidentiality, managed care, forensic topics, dual relationships, and standard of care—all had subgroupings that are worth mentioning.

*Percent of **Total** Responses*

Confidentiality (for Profession)	**58%**
In managed care, managed-care records, utilization review	21%
Regarding computers, faxes, technology	7%
Regarding disclosure in court, subpoenas, raw test data	7%
Regarding other third parties (e.g., family requests)	5%
Group/marriage counseling	3%
Therapy in small towns	3%
Privacy statutes, competence to release information,	

adequacy of release process	<3% each
Confidentiality (Own Practice)	**51%**
Managed care, MCO records intrusion	11%
Information release, subpoenas, test-data disclosure	9%
Couples/family therapy	8%
Computers. fax, technology	4%
Infractions of treatment alliance, reporting laws, insurance requirements, small-town rumors, clinicians talking among themselves about patients	<3% each
Managed Care (for Profession)	**51%**
Insufficient care/coverage, coverage depending on diagnosis	32%
Practice constraints	16%
Liability for outcome	11%
Conflict of interest, dual relationships, fear of being dropped from network	11%
Utilization review clerks' decisions, undermining treatment authority	6%
Ethics in MCO settings (e.g., temptation to lie about diagnosis, need)	6%
Abandonment possibility	5%
Insurance release forms	4%
Fraud, meeting chronic patients' needs, denigration of profession, right to choose clinician, restraint of trade, impersonal care	<3% each
Managed Care (Own Practice)	**33%**
Constraints on care, control of care	19%
Competent care/clinicians	9%
Ethics, combating ethical problems	6%
Liability for MCO's "treatment" decisions, poor capitated coverage	5%
Records' inadequacy or intrusion	4%
Reduced reimbursement	4%
Right to choose therapist, intimidation by MCO, misleading or fraudulent patient	

contracts, misleading or fraudulent clinician contracts,
inadequate/impersonal care   <3% each

Forensic Topics (for Profession)   **42%**

Child custody (evaluation, testimony,
medication from medical doctors)   9%

Competence/competency   7%

Need for forensic training   5%

Court qualifications, expert testimony, experts "for hire"   4%

Juvenile offenders   4%

Being forced to testify, having therapy records subpoenaed   4%

Insanity defense, sexual predator issues/evaluations,
jury selection, assessing pain/suffering/damages   <3% each

Forensic Topics (Own Practice)   **28%**

Child custody evaluations   9%

Testimony in general (divorces, about verdict,
constraints)   7%

Juvenile offenders (including waivers, "punishment")   6%

Child custody and visitation (not formal evaluations)   5%

Competence   5%

Attorney/judge requests, expectations, understanding of
testing/treatment   4%

Need for forensic training   4%

Being forced to testify about therapy, being called
as patient's witness, "patients" using treatment to
file/support lawsuit, insanity defense, sexual predator
evaluations, assessing pain/suffering/damages   <3% each

Dual Relationships/Agency (for Profession)   **23%**

Subgroups were difficult to differentiate, but included bureaucratic
and insurance issues, clinical versus forensic roles, assessment versus treatment roles, role clarity and notification, reporting laws,
clinical versus insurance needs, involvement in patients' legal cases,
and work in small practice communities (e.g., small towns, but also
relatively closed environments, such as universities and prisons).

Dual Relationships/Agency (Own Practice)   **9%**

The subgroups were similar to those for the profession.

Competence, Standard of Care/Training/Supervision (for Profession)	**21%**
Liability for the standard of care with managed care, large caseloads	7%
Suicidal patients	7%
Supervisee's patients	3%
Adequate teaching (clinical and ethics), accidentally falling below the standard, recognizing problem colleagues, responsibility for co-treaters/covering clinicians	<3% each
Competence, Standard of Care/Training /Supervision (Own Practice)	**14%**
Coordinating team approaches/treatments/competencies	5%
Staying within one's areas of competence, specific ethics topics, accidentally falling below the standard, standardizing evaluation and diagnosis	<3% each

Litigious patients were a common practice concern (11%), but less commonly mentioned as a broad professional one. Many respondents reported fears of false allegations or frivolous lawsuits (especially by patients whose personal or family problems, in one person's words, "just can't be fixed"), alleged implantation of false memories, difficulty referring troublesome patients or those with controversial diagnoses, collecting past-due accounts, and "patients" who come to therapy as part of a plan to file (or support) a lawsuit.

Finally, I was impressed that respondents seemed concerned about the effects of these issues on their *patients*. Fear of lawsuit, liability, or misunderstanding was prominent, but more responses were couched in terms of effects on patient care than of dangers for clinicians. That speaks well of the psychotherapy and counseling professions.

APPENDIX B

FORMS USED IN CLINICAL AND FORENSIC PRACTICE

Note: The following examples of forms and letters *must not* be construed as meeting any legal requirement or purpose. They are offered to assist the reader in considering his or her own format for such documents. Although they may be copied without copyright infringement, the author *strongly recommends* that they be modified to meet your specific needs if you decide to use them.

■ ■ ■

CONSENT FOR RELEASE OF INFORMATION

RELEASE OF INFORMATION

I, _____, hereby authorize and request that
Dr._____ release the following information:

_____

_____

_____

to _____

_____

_____

for the purpose of _____

_____

This authorization will expire 30 days from the date below, unless revoked by me. I understand that if I revoke this authorization in the future, information which has already been released in good faith will be considered to have been authorized by me. I also understand that this authorization includes information which may be generated or discovered after I have signed it (but before it expires or is revoked).

A copy of this release shall be as valid as the original.

I have had an opportunity to discuss this authorization with Dr._____ or a member of his (her) staff, and I understand it.

_____ Date _____
_____ Date _____
Witness

DISABILITY INFORMATION RELEASE TO TREATING CLINICIAN

(Sometimes a Social Security disability evaluee wants his or her treating doctor to receive a copy of the disability evaluation [and sometimes it appears to be in the evaluee's interest to recommend it]. *Note that this should not be done in most other kinds of evaluations, although you probably have some duty to communicate findings that threaten life or limb to some appropriate clinician, other person, or agency.* Note also that this is a release to clinicians with a professional interest in the evaluee's case; it is not intended for any other purpose. Although the Social Security Disability Determination Section will also forward evaluation results to treating clinicians if the claimant authorizes it, the process is quite slow and may not be reliable.)

AUTHORIZATION TO RELEASE EVALUATION INFORMATION

I hereby authorize Dr._____ or his (her) associate(s) to release complete information concerning my psychiatric (psychological) evaluation to the physicians and/or mental health professionals who may be providing services to me. This authorization includes Dr. _____'s evaluation report and whatever additional clinical findings and/or recommendations he(she) may wish to communicate, so long as he(she) believes they are in my clinical interest.

The medical or mental health professional(s) authorized to receive the above information are

_____

_____

_____

_____

_____Witness Signature _____

_____Date   Printed Name_____

CONFIDENTIALITY/PRIVACY AGREEMENT FOR ASSOCIATES AND EMPLOYEES

(This form, or one like it, is useful for different kinds of associates, including vendors. It does not take the place of appropriate credentialling, background checks, training, and/or education.)

CONFIDENTIALITY/PRIVACY AGREEMENT

In return for the opportunity to work for or do business with Dr. _____, I, _____, agree to the following regarding confidentiality and privacy:

1. All information that comes to my knowledge or attention, now or in the future, related to Dr. _____, his(her) patients or clients, his(her) practice, or his(her) affairs, including forensic cases, will be kept strictly confidential. It will not be divulged except to persons authorized by Dr. _____ to receive such information.

2. All information or records, whether in physical files, audio- or videotape, computer, or other medium, will be protected against unauthorized access. If a breach of protection occurs, Dr. _____ will be notified within one day of its discovery.

3. No information or records, whether in physical files, audio- or videotape, computer, or other medium, will be copied or removed from the office without authorization. Copies will be treated with the same care as originals.

4. Access to certain materials (such as patient records or "discoverable" and "work product" files) is governed by special legal provisions. I will be sensitive to these requirements, insofar as I am aware of them, and will follow the law as best I can.

5. I understand that attorneys and other persons are often authorized to receive case-related information. I will take reasonable steps to ver-

ify authorization before providing information or documents, and will refer questionable requests to Dr. _____.

6. I understand that breaches of the letter or spirit of this Agreement pose a danger to patient or client well-being, individual reputations and interests, and the fair outcome of legal cases, and, further, may be against the law.

7. This Agreement continues whether or not I continue to work for or with Dr. _____, and extends indefinitely into the future.

8. I have had an opportunity to ask questions about any portions of this Agreement I may not fully understand, and I have received a copy for my files. *I accept the fact that if I do not sign, and abide by, this Agreement, my employment and/or business relationship with Dr. _____ may be terminated immediately.*

_____Signature

_____Printed name   _____Date

_____Witness for Dr._____ _____Date

Vendor Confidentiality/Professionalism Agreement

(This is an agreement that may be useful for such vendors as answering services or, with some modification, temporary help agencies.)

CONFIDENTIALITY AGREEMENT

In consideration of our performing telephone answering and related services for Dr. _____, the _____ Telephone Answering Service ("Service") agrees to the following regarding privacy and confidentiality.

1. "Service" includes any and all persons working for _____ Telephone Answering Service (whether employees, contractors, or other), its agents, and all persons with access to its records, client lists, messages, equipment, or telephone lines.

2. All information that comes to the Service, now or at any time in the future, related to Dr. _____'s patients or practice will be kept strictly confidential, and not divulged to any person except Dr. _____, his(her) authorized employees, or other persons whom he(she) has authorized, in writing, to receive such information.

3. All information or records, whether in physical files, computer memory, or any other storage medium, will be protected against unauthorized access. Should a breach of that protection occur, Dr. _____ will be notified within one business day of discovering the breach.

4. This Agreement continues whether or not the Service continues to do business with Dr. _____, and will apply to any future company or answering service that may purchase or merge with the current Service.

5. This Agreement is not meant to impede communication between the Service and Dr. _____'s office. Nevertheless, the Service will take

reasonable steps to verify the identity of any person purporting to represent Dr. _____ before disclosing messages or other information.

_____ Owner, _____ Telephone

Answering Service

_____Printed name

_____ Date

_____for Dr._____

INITIAL ATTORNEY AGREEMENT LETTER (FORENSIC PRACTICE)

(I don't require that attorneys actually sign a "letter of agreement"; however, many forensic professionals do.)

Date _____

_____ , Attorney

_____

_____

TO: _____

RE:_____

Dear _____

This will follow up our telephone conversation, in which we talked briefly about _____ _____. I should be pleased to examine the details and consult with you regarding my findings. As we discussed, my review will be objective, and I have not represented to you that my findings will be helpful to your case.

The next step would be a review of relevant medical/psychological records and other relevant facts, materials, and litigants' contentions. These may be sent to the address above.

Enclosed please find a *curriculum vitae* and a statement of fees and charges. My retainer is $_____. Accounts are billed every thirty days.

Please note that this letter does not constitute an agreement for services until either a retainer is accepted or such an agreement is established in writing.

Cordially,

_____

STATEMENT OF FEES AND CHARGES (FORENSIC PRACTICE)

(This kind of information is very important to the relationship between you and the person or organization that retains you. I strongly recommend that some similar document be a part of your initial correspondence and that you keep a copy with the case file. Of course, your specific fees and working arrangements are up to you, and are not meant to be dictated or influenced by this form.)

FORENSIC FEES AND CHARGES AS OF (MONTH), (YEAR)

Please read this document carefully before contracting for services.

The following are fees and charges established on____(date) for forensic services and related activities performed by _____. **All fees are assumed to be guaranteed by the retaining individual, company, agency, or jurisdiction, at the rates below. The client agrees to bear all costs of collecting overdue accounts unless otherwise agreed in writing by Dr. _____.** I am not expected to bill any patient, family member, insurance company, or litigant unless specifically arranged in advance, in writing. All consultation and financial agreements are with the contracting consultee, agency, or jurisdiction alone.

Consultations will be considered without regard to whether they are related to the defense or plaintiff in civil cases, or the defense or prosecution in criminal cases.

Fees. All professional activities, including but not necessarily limited to record or case review, interview, examination, conference (in-person or by telephone), report preparation, travel time ("door-to-door"), testimony, and time spent waiting, are charged by the hour, at a maximum of $____ **per hour.**

Per diem charges are a maximum of $_____ **per day, plus expenses.** For partial days, the consultee will be charged the lesser of the total hourly fees (at the relevant rates above) or $_____. Time will be measured from leaving home or office, until return to home or office. If time is spent in work on other professional matters, it will be subtracted from the total.

A retainer of $_____ is usually required. No obligation or agreement for services exists until either a retainer is accepted or an agreement to proceed without retainer is established in writing. In some cases, an additional, refundable deposit or credit balance may be required after the retainer has been depleted.

Accounts are billed every thirty days, net due upon receipt of statement. **Note:** Payment of any outstanding balance is expected before testimony, and a minimum pretestimony deposit may be required.

Consultations will not be accepted on any "contingency" basis, nor will fees be adjusted in any way that is related to the outcome of a case.

Unkept appointments not canceled more than 48 hours in advance may be charged at the regular rate, unless filled with other gainful activity. **Time will not be "double-billed."**

All expenses are additional. Air and rail travel will be first-class unless prohibited by government rule; all "coach" fares will be at a "changeable and refundable" rate. Automobile rental will be billed at "mid-sized" rates; private automobile travel at $ 0.__ per mile. Accommodations will be in business-class hotels or motels, with a food allowance of $___ per day. **Alcoholic beverages and entertainment will not be billed to clients.**

"Emergency" consultation or work with less than seven days' notice is subject to a 50% surcharge.

Statements will be itemized, with copies of receipts attached. Original time sheets, billing notes, etc., will be provided upon request.

PRE-EVALUATION UNDERSTANDING

(This is a form I ask evaluees to sign before disability or forensic evaluations. It is a complement to documented discussion of the same topics. The type is purposely large, and I explain it as necessary. One copy is filed, and one given to the evaluee.)

UNDERSTANDING YOUR FORENSIC PSYCHIATRY EVALUATION

I, _____, understand that I am seeing Dr. _____ solely for psychiatric (psychological, etc.) evaluation. The purpose of my evaluation is legal or administrative, not treatment or treatment-related diagnosis. This means that Dr. _____ is not "my doctor (psychologist, therapist)," and this evaluation does not create a doctor–patient (clinician–patient, therapist–patient) relationship with Dr. _____.

I understand that the things that I discuss with Dr. _____ are not confidential in the same way that a "doctor–patient" interview might be. For example, Dr. _____ may write a report for a court, attorney, or other person or organization that is entitled to information about my evaluation. Dr. _____ may also be asked to testify in court or at deposition about his findings or the things I discuss in the evaluation. Nevertheless, I understand that I should try to cooperate in the interview as best I can, and be honest and straightforward in my answers.

A copy of this statement will be given to me to keep, and I may ask questions of Dr. _____ at any time during the evaluation. If I have questions after the evaluation, they should be referred to my attorney.

_____ Date _____
Evaluee

_____ Date _____
Witness

Documenting Evaluee Status Before Evaluation

(This is information from the first page of my general evaluation/examination format. It summarizes some of the information I like to document before proceeding.)

Date(s) of Evaluation
Purpose
Eval. setting   Agency/Comment
Referral source
Notifications/disclaimers__Purpose   __Confidentiality limits
                          __Agency   __Report/testify possibility
Does evaluee understand the above notifications/disclaimers?
                                              Y___ N___
Evaluee signature on:
                __Forensic understanding __Other, for _____
Seen with:
Other persons present
Evaluee's primary language/communication
Type of action/litigation
Evaluee's role in action/litigation
Other

All information on this form is from the evaluee unless otherwise noted. Other sources of corroborating information, records, depositions, etc., are generally not reflected on this form.

GLOSSARY OF COMMON LEGAL AND FORSENIC TERMS

ACTIONABLE: Giving rise to a "cause of action," i.e., referring to something for which one may file suit (e.g., "actionable negligence").

ACTUS REUS: The behavioral part of a crime; that which is physically done (see *"Mens rea"*).

ADVOCACY: In legal terms, the active espousing of a legal cause. The forensic expert should not be the litigant's advocate, but may argue for his or her (i.e., the expert's) opinions. This is different from the duty of advocacy expected when a treating clinician acts in the interests of his or her patient/client.

AGENCY: A relationship in which a person acts on behalf of, and with some authority from, another person or organization.

AGENT: A person who acts on behalf of another, or an organization, with a mutual agreement to do so.

ALIENATION OF AFFECTIONS: A tort (civil wrong) arising from the willful and malicious interference with a marriage relationship by some third party. Abolished in many states, it still may be raised in some when therapy (or a therapist) is accused of interfering with a patient's marriage.

AMICUS CURIAE: An outside person or organization (i.e., one not involved as a litigant) who brings a matter of interest to the court's attention when it might otherwise be overlooked. (Note that this phrase does not apply to expert or fact witnesses, a common misunderstanding among clinicians.)

APPELLANT: The party who appeals a court decision—always the party not satisfied with the immediately prior ruling in the judicial process. The appellant's name is placed first in the legal citation ("styling") of the case, regardless of the original wording.

APPELLATE COURT: A court whose jurisdiction allows it to review cases already tried. (Note that an appeal is not a new trial, but a review of the legal matters involved in a previous one. The appellate court may sometimes authorize a new trial in a *trial* court.)

APPELLEE: The party who defends against an appeal—always the party that is satisfied with the immediately prior ruling in the judicial process.

APPORTION: Among other definitions, to divide in some fair way, such as to apportion blame between two unsuccessful defendants in a malpractice lawsuit.

APPRECIATE: Among other definitions, to go beyond factual "knowing" to useful understanding, as in a mentally ill person's being able to appreciate the difference between right and wrong, not merely to quote it,

A PRIORI: A way of arriving at a conclusion about something by assuming that it logically must flow from some other, established fact. (For example, "Ms. Jones had her left arm amputated when she was a child. Thus one can assume *a priori* that she was not the bandit observed holding a pistol with two hands.")

ARRAIGN: To accuse of a wrong. **Arraignment** is the first step in the criminal accusation process, at which the defendant is formally charged and presented with an "accusatory instrument," informed of his or her rights, offered an opportunity to plead, provided with counsel if he or she can afford none, etc.

ASSAULT: An attempt, with unlawful force, to injure another person, in a circumstance under which injury is probable if not prevented (note that actual touching is not required).

ASSUMPTION OF RISK: In civil law, an act in which the injured party knows he or she might be injured and voluntarily places himself or herself at risk anyway. (That includes, for example, the patient who refuses an assessment or treatment procedure after the risks of not having it done have been appropriately explained. The person's assumption of the risks of not having the procedure are a defense that the clinician may raise in any later negligence [e.g., malpractice] suit related to the person's not receiving the procedure.)

BATTERY: The unlawful touching, or "application of force," to another. Battery need not result in physical injury, and may exist even if only an extension of the person is touched (e.g., his or her car).

BEYOND A REASONABLE DOUBT: See **"Burden of proof."**

BONA FIDE: In good faith, genuine, without fraud or deceit.

BREACH: In law, a failure to perform some duty or obligation.

BRIEF: In law, a written argument provided to a court that sets out legal points and authorities.

BURDEN OF PROOF: The weight of the evidence that a complainant, petitioner, or accuser must show to the trier of fact that the matter being considered actually occurred. In a criminal trial, the burden is "beyond a reasonable doubt" (extremely sure, generally 95–98%); in most civil trials, a mere "preponderance of the evidence" (just over 50%); and in some civil settings, such as child custody and most civil commitments, "clear and convincing evidence" (some level about midway between the other two, depending on state or federal statute).

CALUMNY: Slander, defamation, false prosecution (an old term).

CANON: A rule of ecclesiastical law, but also a rule or standard of conduct adopted by a professional organization for its members.

CAPITAL OFFENSE: (Capital murder, capital crime) An offense punishable by death.

CAUSE OF ACTION: A legal claim sufficient to demand judicial attention.

CERTIORARI: (*Writ of certiorari*) Agreement by an appellate court to review the decision of a lower court. In state courts, this is sometimes called "certification."

CODICIL: A supplement to a will that changes the will in some way. Demands the same competence as the will itself.

COMITY: A courtesy extended by one state or jurisdiction to recognize the decisions of another with concomitant jurisdiction. Not a matter of law, but of agreement.

COMMON LAW: A system of jurisprudence, and part of the overall legal system, that is based on judicial precedent rather than on statute. Originally based on unwritten law of England, it relies on principles that may be flexible and evolve, rather than on specifics and absolutes.

COMMUTATION: Substitution of a lesser criminal sentence for a greater one, as in commuting a sentence to "time served" or commuting a death sentence to some period of incarceration.

COMPETENT: Capable of doing a particular thing. Competence is not generic, but is tied to the task to which it is being applied (e.g., competence to make a will, to stand trial, to consent to a particular treatment).

COMPOS MENTIS: Mentally competent.

CONCLUSION OF FACT: A legal conclusion based solely on the facts and so-called "natural reasoning," without relying on rules of law.

CONCLUSION OF LAW: A legal conclusion (by a judge) reached solely by the application of rules of law, regardless of the facts. Used when the ultimate conclusion cannot reasonably be reached by applying the facts of a case (e.g., when there are insufficient facts).

CONFESSION: An admission of guilt. In order to be valid in a criminal court, a confession must be accompanied by a number of legal elements, such as competence to make a confession, understanding of one's rights, and voluntariness.

CONSENT: In mental health law, the legal agreeing of one person to an act or procedure by another in which the first person participates. Valid consent has elements of knowledge (cf., "informed consent"), *competence* to make the consent, and voluntariness or freedom from undue influence.

CONSERVATOR: A temporary guardian of property appointed by a court of proper jurisdiction.

CONSULTANT: In clinical professions, a person called upon by a primary caregiver to advise him or her regarding a patient or patient care. The consultant's professional relationship is with the person who contracted for his or her services (the **consultee**), and not generally with the patient; thus a clinician–patient relationship may not form.

CONTEMPT OF COURT: An act or omission that tends to interfere with, or obstruct, the orderly conduct of justice, or to impair the respect for and dignity of the court. Contempt of court need not actually occur in a courtroom.

CONTINGENCY (CONTINGENT) FEE: In law or forensic professions, a fee for services that depends on the outcome of a case; unethical for forensic experts.

CONTRACTOR, INDEPENDENT: One who makes an agreement with someone to do a piece of work, but retains control of the means, method, and manner of production.

CORONER: A public official who investigates and rules on causes and circumstances of death. A coroner need not be a physician.

CORPUS DELICTI: "Body of the crime," a prima facie showing that a crime has been committed. In a prosecution for murder, for example, a showing that the death was due to a criminal act. Does not apply only to murder, and does not refer solely to a "dead body."

COURT MARTIAL: A military tribunal with jurisdiction over crimes against the law of the Armed Services. There are several differences between civilian (criminal) courts and courts martial. Courts martial, like all other U.S. courts, are subservient to the U.S. Constitution.

CRUEL AND UNUSUAL PUNISHMENT: A flexible term usually taken to mean punishment found to be offensive to an ordinary person (i.e., to ordinary society, not just to one person).

DAMAGES: In civil law, monetary compensation designed to right a wrong or, under special circumstances, to punish one who commits a civil wrong (exemplary or punitive damages). Sometimes damages awarded are "nominal" or trivial, to indicate that the plaintiff is technically in the right but does not require or deserve compensation.

DAUBERT RULE: A rule regarding the admissibility of expert or research evidence, limiting it to evidence with scientific merit and not "junk science." Has generally replaced the Frye test.

DECLARATORY JUDGMENT: A court decision that establishes a litigant's right or expresses a court opinion, but does not require that anything further be done by the parties. Often used when the parties are expected to resolve further matters themselves.

DEFAMATION: Illegal publication of something injurious about one's "good name" or reputation. When oral, it is *slander;* when written or designed to be read, it is *libel.*

DEFENDANT: One who is accused by a **plaintiff** in a civil action, or who is accused of a crime in a **criminal** action.

DELIBERATE INDIFFERENCE: See **"Reckless disregard."**

DEPONENT: A witness who gives information under oath during a **deposition**.

DEPOSITION: A pretrial discovery process that allows adversarial questioning by one side of the witnesses for the other, under oath, in an environment governed by courtlike rules. May be oral or written ("deposition by written interrogatories").

DIRECTED VERDICT: A jury verdict that is brought at the direction of the judge, often because of some legally incontrovertible matter of law. May occur when there is a *prima facie* case, or when an opposing party fails to make such a case. In criminal trials, there can be a directed verdict of acquittal, but not of "guilty."

DISCHARGE: Among other definitions, a description of methods by which a legal duty is extinguished.

DISCLOSURE: Among other definitions, see **"Discovery."**

DISCOVERY: A pretrial procedure in which, subject to legal rules, the opposing parties in a litigation are allowed access to important information about each other's case. The making available of information to which the other side is entitled is called **disclosure,** and may occur in **deposition** or **interrogatory.**

DISCRETION: Reasonable exercise of a power or right to act in an official capacity. In clinical settings, may be applied to a clinician-employee's freedom to act in a patient's best interest, or flexibility to make decisions regarding care. Involves choice and will, so that **discretionary duties** are those in which a nurse, counselor, or doctor, for example, may (and may have a responsibility to) legitimately and flexibly rely on his or her professional ability to act as he or she thinks best.

DUCES TECUM: See *"Subpoena duces tecum."*

DUE CARE: The standard of care or legal duty owed to another, the absence of which defines **negligence.** Often involves consideration of *reasonableness*, or a *reasonable* clinician or person.

DUE PROCESS: (Due process of law) A Constitutional concept mentioned in the Fifth and Fourteenth Amendments. Not specifically defined, but refers to fundamental fairness in legal and government procedures. Divided in legal discussions into *substantive* and *procedural* components.

DURESS: Involuntary external influence over an action, such as to force one to commit an otherwise criminal act or influence one to consent to a medical procedure. Duress can remove the voluntariness necessary for an act, such as consent, and remove the intent necessary to define a criminal act.

DURHAM RULE: (also *Product Rule*) A rule for determining criminal responsibility in persons with mental disease or defect, now used in few, if any, jurisdictions. It was quite liberal, allowing lack of responsibility if the act was simply the "product" of such a condition.

DUTY: An obligation of conduct owed by one person or entity to another. In the law of negligence (including malpractice), a duty is a legally sanctioned obligation for which breach results in liability. Clinicians thus must conduct themselves in such a manner as to avoid negligent injury to those to whom they have a duty (including, but not limited to, patients).

EN BANC: Referring to all members of an appellate court hearing a case together, rather than having it heard by only some of the judges.

EQUAL PROTECTION: (Equal protection of/under the law) A Fourteenth Amendment Constitutional guarantee.

ESTOPPEL: A prohibition from denying the truth of a point that has been established in case law, legislation, or one's own acts.

EX PARTE: Referring to action by one litigating party without notice or participation by the other.

EVALUEE: In forensic evaluations, one who is assessed for some purpose other than clinically related evaluation, diagnosis, treatment, or care. Not a **patient.**

EXPERT TESTIMONY: See **"Expert witness."**

EXPERT WITNESS: A witness with "special knowledge" (beyond that of an ordinary person) about the topic about which he or she is to testify. Such a person may testify in ways not allowed for "fact" witnesses, including offering opinions, discussing hypothetical situations, and relying on information other than that which he or she has personally observed. The court must agree that he or she is qualified before "expert" status is bestowed.

EX POST FACTO: Generally referring to the fact that a criminal defendant must be tried under laws in force at the time of the allegedly criminal act. Thus a person convicted of a murder committed when there was no death penalty cannot be sentenced to death under a new law that allows it. It is important to understand that *ex post facto* applies only to criminal law, not to civil matters.

FALSE IMPRISONMENT: The unjustified detention of a person, sufficient to amount to an imprisonment (not mere obstruction), of any appreciable duration. Sometimes seen in cases of wrongful commitment.

FEDERAL TORT CLAIMS ACT: A federal law under which lawsuits for money damages against the federal government are heard, and a general waiver of **sovereign immunity**.

FELONY: A "high crime" as compared with less serious "misdemeanors." Some states define felonies as crimes punishable by death or imprisonment for more than one year. See **"Misdemeanor."**

FIDUCIARY: A person having a duty, created by his or her own undertaking, to act primarily for the benefit of another in all matters connected with that undertaking (e.g., a doctor or therapist has a fiduciary relationship with a patient).

FORESEEABILITY: (e.g., foreseeable risks) A concept that generally limits liability for negligence in that actions may often be deemed negligent only when their injurious consequences are foreseeable.

GRAND JURY: A body of people, part of a court of criminal jurisdiction, that investigates crimes committed and indicts persons accused of them when it discovers sufficient evidence to warrant holding the person for trial. Trial juries are called *petit juries.*

HABEAS CORPUS: A procedure for obtaining a judicial determination of the legality of keeping an individual in legal custody; can be used to determine whether a criminal conviction is consistent with due process of law.

HARMLESS ERROR: In a trial, errors of law that are not sufficiently prejudicial to warrant modification of a lower court decision by an appellate court.

INCOMPETENCE, INCOMPETENCY: See **"Competence."**

INDICTMENT: The formal charging of a person with a crime, submitted to a grand jury.

INFORMED CONSENT: See **"Consent."**

INJUNCTION: A judicial remedy awarded to require a party to refrain from doing something.

IN LOCO PARENTIS: Referring to a person or entity that lawfully takes the place of a parent or guardian for some legal purpose (e.g., the relationship between a minor and a boarding school or hospital).

INQUEST: An inquiry made by a coroner to determine the cause of death of someone who has died under circumstances requiring such investigation (e.g., under suspicious circumstances or in prison).

INSANITY: A legal term connoting an absence of responsibility and defined for some purpose (e.g., criminal responsibility, commitment to a mental institution, ability to stand trial). The term is specifically defined in statute, and should not be confused with a psychiatric or psychological "definition."

INTENT: A state of mind in which the person knows and desires the consequences of his or her act. In most cases of criminal liability, intent must exist at the time the offense is committed. Intent is generally not necessary for civil findings of negligence.

INTERROGATORIES: In civil actions, a pretrial discovery tool in which written questions are served on the opposing side, which must provide written replies under oath.

JUDGMENT ON THE MERITS: A decision or judgment based on the essential facts of the case rather than on a technical rule. A decision on the merits is rendered by the trier of fact (a jury, or in cases with no jury, the judge).

JURY: (petit jury) An ordinary trial jury, a group summoned and sworn to decide the facts (not the law) of an issue at trial. See also **"Grand jury."**

LEADING QUESTION: A question asked by a lawyer at trial or deposition that is improper on direct examination because it suggests to the witness the answer that he or she should deliver. Leading questions are allowed when the witness is one who is defined as "hostile" or an **adverse** witness.

MALICIOUS PROSECUTION: A legal action to recover damages that are the result of unsuccessful criminal or civil proceedings pursued without probable cause and with malice. Lawsuits for malicious prosecution are sometimes brought by former malpractice defendants who believe they have been frivolously sued.

MALPRACTICE: A tort involving, in general, negligent breach of a clinical duty within a clinician–patient relationship. See **"Tort."**

MENS REA: The mental state accompanying a forbidden act. Most commonly used in criminal cases to refer to the defendant's ability to have knowledge and intent regarding his or her act. See also *"Actus rea."*

MENTAL ANGUISH: A compensable injury covering all forms of mental, as opposed to physical, pain (e.g., anxiety, fear, grief). See **"Pain and suffering."**

MISDEMEANOR: A class of criminal offenses that are less serious than felonies and incur less severe penalties. They often are tried in a lesser court than are felony charges, may give rise to fewer procedural safeguards at trial, and conviction may not carry the same disqualifications for future activities (such as holding political office or serving on a jury) as a felony.

MISPRISION OF FELONY: A misdemeanor now largely limited to concealing a felony that has been committed by oneself or someone else; may rarely apply to failing to take reasonable and safe steps to prevent or disclose a felony (e.g., call the police).

MISTRIAL: A trial that is stopped by the judge and declared void prior to a verdict by the fact finder (jury or, in the absence of a jury, judge). It does not result in a judgment for either party, but indicates a failure of the trial.

MITIGATION: Generally modification, although often considered to mean a diminishing of seriousness. *Mitigating circumstances* in a capital murder case, for example, may suggest that the sentence be modified downward because of provocation, or adjusted upward because of particular cruelty. *Mitigation of damages* is a civil term requiring that a person injured by another person's tort or breach exercise reasonable diligence and ordinary care to avoid aggravating the injury or increasing damages.

M'NAGHTEN RULE (McNAUGHTEN): A common law test of criminal responsibility when a defendant, by reason of mental disease or defect, may not be able to distinguish right from wrong. Some jurisdictions add a dimension of "irresistible impulse," in which a person who does know that his or her conduct is wrongful but is unable to resist committing the act can be acquitted. Also known as the *right–wrong test*. Generally replaced in most U.S. jurisdictions with an insanity defense rule based on recommendations of the American Law Institute.

MORAL CERTAINTY: An old term for "beyond a reasonable doubt."

NEGLIGENCE: Failure to exercise that degree of care that a person of ordinary prudence (or a "reasonable person") would exercise under the same circumstances. Negligence does not require intent. General negligence does not imply reckless disregard for the interests of others. *Contributory negligence* is conduct on the part of the plaintiff that falls below the standard to which he or she should conform for his or her own protection, and that is a legally contributing cause to any damage resulting from the defendant's negligence (cf.,

"Assumption of risk"). *Gross negligence* is failure to use even slight care (as contrasted with ordinary negligence, which is failure to use ordinary care).

NOLO CONTENDERE: A statement that a defendant will not contest a charge made by the government. The statement (not really a plea) is often made to resolve a criminal situation, and may be used to avoid civil effects from criminal cases.

NONSUIT: A judgment rendered against a plaintiff who fails to proceed to trial or is unable to prove his or her case. It does not decide the merits of the case, and thus does not preclude the plaintiff's bringing the suit again.

PAIN AND SUFFERING: A kind of damages that a person may recover for physical or mental discomfort that results from a wrong against him or her.

PATIENT: One with whom a clinician forms a relationship for the purpose of clinical evaluation, diagnosis, treatment, or care. A fiduciary relationship is present between clinician and patient. It also exists if the person is called something else (e.g., "client"), so long as the purpose of the relationship is the same. Different from **Evaluee**, although if an evaluee has reason to believe, or is led to believe, that he or she is a patient, a special duty may sometimes be created.

PLAINTIFF: One who initially brings a suit. When called a "plaintiff in error," refers to one who appeals a lower court judgment against him or her (whether he or she was the plaintiff or defendant in the lower court).

PLEADINGS: Legal statements of the facts that constitute a plaintiff's cause of action and a defendant's grounds for defense.

POLICE POWER: The power that state and local governments have to impose restrictions on private rights when those restrictions are reasonably related to government interests (including maintenance of the general public welfare). Civil commitment laws are based in the police powers of the state, and no longer in its parental responsibility (*parens patriae* responsibility).

PRECEDENT: A case or rule in case law that is recognized as an authority for the disposition of future cases. Only appellate cases can create precedent. Precedent is created only in the jurisdiction covered by the appellate court that made the decision.

PRELIMINARY HEARING: In criminal law, a means of determining whether or not probable cause for an arrest existed; held prior to the issuance of an indictment.

***PRIMA FACIE* CASE:** A case sufficient on its face, but supported by at least a minimum of evidence, to go to a jury; one that will usually prevail in the absence of evidence to the contrary. See also *"Res ipsa loquitur."*

PRIVILEGE: With regard to "confidentiality," the right of an individual to limit and/or direct the use of information about himself or herself under certain circumstances. Related to "privileged communication" between a person and another person with an obligation (duty) of confidentiality.

PROXIMATE CAUSE: A term used in negligence cases to indicate a natural and continuous, unbroken sequence between an event (such as a breach of a duty) and an injury, generally without which the injury would not have occurred.

REASONABLE CERTAINTY: (Reasonable [medical, psychological, psychiatric, professional] certainty) Defined differently in different jurisdictions, and sometimes differently for criminal and civil cases (with more certainty for criminal matters); often not defined in statute at all. Should not be confused with the certainty necessary to make a diagnosis or to choose a particular treatment, or with the several burdens of proof (preponderance, etc.).

RECKLESS DISREGARD: Describing an act or conduct without concern for the consequences, especially heedless of danger; often "wanton disregard" or "deliberate indifference" to consequences. It implies a defendant's consciousness of a danger and a willingness to assume a risk. Thus when reckless disregard (or "deliberate indifference") occurs with negligence, the level of negligence is often increased (e.g., to "gross negligence"). It does not necessarily require criminal intent to harm.

REMAND: In appeals cases, to send back for further trial or deliberation.

RES IPSA LOQUITUR: Literally, "the thing speaks for itself"; a rule whereby negligence may be inferred simply from the fact that an accident happened because the negligence is so obvious that one cannot reasonably contest it. Amputation of the wrong limb is sometimes used as a general example.

RESPONDEAT SUPERIOR: A doctrine of relying on a "master" or employer to assume liability for the **torts** of an employee or an agent (servant).

REVERSIBLE ERROR: An error of law during a trial that substantially affects the legal rights of the person who lost, and that, if uncorrected, would result in a miscarriage of justice. Thus an appellate court may reverse a lower court decision based on reversible error, but not on **harmless error**. Also called prejudicial error.

RIGHT–WRONG TEST: See "**M'Naghten Rule**."

SETTLEMENT: The conclusive resolution of a legal matter. In civil suits, a compromise achieved before final judgment that eliminates the necessity of a judicial resolution.

SOVEREIGN IMMUNITY: A doctrine that precludes suits against a sovereign government—when the government is engaged in an official function—without the government's consent. Today governments have granted, through various actions, a number of exceptions to the old rule of sovereign immunity. Other exceptions have been created by judicial decision.

STARE DECISIS: The rule by which common law courts are reluctant to interfere with the principles found in former decisions, and may uphold those principles even though the court might decide otherwise if the question were slightly different. This is the general reason that our judicial system overturns earlier precedents only on showing of good cause, rather than bringing similar cases to trial.

STATUTE OF LIMITATIONS: Generally refers to any law that creates a time limit during which a person must bring a judicial action or else be barred from such an action in the future. Very serious criminal acts may have no statute of limitations. The statute of limitations for things such as malpractice liability is generally about two years from the time that a damage was discovered. "Hidden" damage and damage to a minor are two conditions that can substantially increase the statute of limitations (or, more properly, delay the beginning of the period being measured).

STRICT LIABILITY: Liability without showing fault. Often used in **tort** law when one can show an obvious and inherent risk of injury (e.g., one who uses explosives is likely to be liable for all resulting injuries, even if he or she exercises the utmost care). Strict liability tends to discourage dangerous activities, while not entirely prohibiting them.

SUBPOENA: A writ issued under authority of a court to compel appearance at a judicial proceeding, the disobedience of which may be a *contempt of court.* A subpoena *duces tecum* requires the subpoenaed individual to bring relevant documents or materials to trial (or deposition).

SUMMARY JUDGMENT: A preverdict judgment rendered by the court in response to a motion by either side (in a civil case) that claims that the facts are so strong in its favor that there is no need for a jury trial because there can be no real dispute about the facts, or because only a question of law is involved.

TERM OF ART: Words or terms that have a particular meaning to a specific area of study, such as some diagnostic terms for mental health professionals, which have a different meaning, or no meaning, outside that context.

TORT: A private or civil "wrong" resulting from a breach of a legal duty. **Malpractice** is a civil tort. A tort consists of four essential elements: a legal duty owed by the defendant to the plaintiff, breach (dereliction) of that duty, damage to the plaintiff, and a causal relationship between the breach and the damage. A *tort-feasor* is one who commits a tort. Conduct that subjects one to tort liability is said to be *tortious*.

TRIBUNAL: An officer or body having the authority to adjudicate matters.

TRIER OF FACT: In a trial, the body or person responsible for deciding whether or not the facts (evidence) presented by each side support that side to the extent required by the relevant burden or proof. In a *jury* trial, the trier of fact is always the jury. In a *bench* trial, it is the judge.

TRIER OF LAW: In a trial, the judge, who determines whether or not matters of law have been met and legal processes followed in the trial. When there is no jury, the judge is also the **trier of fact**.

UNDUE INFLUENCE: Influence of another that destroys one's free will or free agency. In mental health issues, often relates to issues of consent or clinician impropriety.

VOIR DIRE: Literally, "to speak the truth." Usually refers to an examination by attorneys or the court of prospective jurors to determine their qualifications for jury service in a particular matter. Experts may also be *"voir dired,"* as may other individuals, out of the presence of the jury, when an initial determination about their qualifications or appropriateness must be made before presentation to the jury.

WITNESS: One who gives evidence in a cause before a court under oath. A **fact witness** is one who is allowed to testify on matters that he or she personally knows or has observed. An **expert witness** is one who is allowed to give opinions and to testify in other special ways based on his or her special knowledge or qualifications to assist the court in a complex matter. An **adverse** or **hostile witness** is one whose relationship to the opposing party may prejudice his or her testimony. A witness declared to be hostile may be asked leading questions and is subject to cross-examination by the party who calls him or her.

WORDS OF ART: See **"Term of art."**

WORKER'S COMPENSATION: Refers to laws that generally establish the liability of employers for injuries or illnesses that arise as a result of, and in the course of, employment. The liability is specifically created without regard to fault or negligence, and is designed to provide reasonable medical care and compensation for loss of income without subjecting either the worker or the employer to a lawsuit.

WORK PRODUCT: Work done by an attorney in the process of representing a client; ordinarily not subject to discovery.

WRIT: A mandatory precept issued by the authority of, and in the name of, a government for the purpose of compelling a person to do something.

WRIT OF CERTIORARI*:** See ***"Certiorari."

APPENDIX D

FURTHER RESOURCES

JOURNALS

Behavioral Sciences and the Law
Journal of the American Academy of Psychiatry and the Law
Law and Human Behavior

BOOKS

Behnke, S.H., et al. (1998). *The Essentials of California Mental Health Law*. New York: Norton. (*Essentials of Massachusetts Mental Health Law* is also available from Norton, with others apparently scheduled to follow.)

Berger, S. (1997). *Establishing a Forensic Psychiatric Practice*. New York: Norton.

Deyoub, P., & Douthit, G. (1996). *A Practical Guide to Forensic Psychology*, New York: Jason Aronson.

Lifson, L.E., & Simon, R.I. (1998). *The Mental Health Practitioner and the Law: A Comprehensive Handbook* (section on "The Clinician in Court"). Cambridge, MA: Harvard University Press.

Several books on the forensic uses of standard psychometric instruments, such as: McCann, J.T., & Dyer, F.J. (1996). *Forensic Assessment with the Millon Inventories*. New York: Guilford.

■ ■ ■

WEB SITES

(Be careful; information on private Web sites is often unverified or unreliable. I do not warrant the quality or accuracy of any information obtained from the Internet.) All of the Web sites below were active as of late 1998. Many have links to others with information about the law, courts, court decisions, organizations, individual practitioners, and so on. Internet searches, such as <+psychology +forensic>, will produce many hits.

American Academy of Forensic Psychology
   <http://www.abfp.com/>
American Academy of Psychiatry and the Law
   <http://www.cc.emory.edu/AAPL/>
Forensic Nursing Resource Homepage
   <http://wkweb4.cableinet.co.uk/pwoods1/index.html>
Forensic Psychiatry Resources, Myron Pulier, M.D.
   <http://www.umdnj.edu/psyevnts/forensic.html>
Forensic Psychiatry, Harold Bursztajn, M.D.
   <http://www.forensic-psych.com>
Forensic Psychology and Psychiatry
   <http://www.geocities.com/Athens/7429/psychlaw.html>
Forensic Psychology and Psychiatry Links, David Wilshire
   <http://www.ozemail.com.au/~dwillsh/>
Forensic Psychology Database
   <http://flash.lakeheadu.ca/~pals/forensics/index.html>
Forensic Science Resources, Carpenter
   <http://www.tncrimlaw.com/forensic/>
Psychiatry and Law Resources, Hooper
   <http://ua1vm.ua.edu/~jhooper/>
Psychiatry and Law Updates, William Reid, M.D., M.P.H.
   <http://www.reidpsychiatry.com>
Psychology and the Law (Selected Topics)
   <http://www.users.cts.com/king/h/hflowe/>
"So you want to be a forensic psychologist?"
   <http://www.geocities.com/Athens/7429/forensicpsychprep.html>

University of Virginia Institute of Law, Psychiatry and Public Policy
  <http://ness.sys.Virginia.EDU/ilppp/>
Zeno's Forensic Page
  <http://zeno.simplenet.com/forensic.html>

INDEX

Abandonment, 34-35, 60-61
Accepting patients, 32-34, 58-59
Advance directives, 79
Adversarial system, 17
Adverse effects:
  disclosure of, 77
  of treatment, 129-132
Advertising, 39-40
Agency, 21, 66
"Alternative" biological
  treatments, 72-73
American Civil Liberties Union
  (ACLU), 29*n*
American Psychiatric Association,
  7, 25, 109, 120
American Psychological
  Association, 7, 25, 120
Appeals, 146
Assent, 78
Assessment:
  of dangerousness, 109-111
  of suicide risk, 100
Availability, 11
Awareness of suicide risk, 99

Barter payment arrangements, 60
Billing, 59-60
Biological treatments,
  "alternative," 72-73

Books, 186
Boundary violations, 80-90
  nonsexual, 87-90
  sexual. *See* Sexual boundary
    violations
Breach of duty, 25
Burden of proof, 17-18

Case-limited supervision, 50-51
Causation, 25
Causes of action, 26
Children:
  evaluations of, 138
  records of, 92-93
Clinical evaluation, 32
Clinically recommending, 73
Clinical practice, 5-14
  availability, 11
  consultation. *See* Consultation
  continuing education, 8
  co-treatment, 9, 10
  countertransference
    vulnerability, 6-7
  documentation, 12-13
  ethical guidelines, 7
  family contact, 13-14
  moral guidelines, 7-8
  reputation, 14
  supervision, 8-10

therapeutic correctness, 10-11
training and credentials, 5-6
working while impaired, 14
Clinical standards of care, 24-25,
31-42
advertising and, 39-40
dangerousness assessment and,
109-111
vs. financial limitations, 31-35
vs. instructions from employers
or contractors, 35
least restrictive clinically appropriate alternative,
41-42
managed care and, 70
vs. patient requests or social
pressure, 36-37
vs. policies or guidelines, 38–39
practicing outside or beyond
primary qualifications,
37-38
variation in duty related to type
of patient relationship, 40-41
Clinician-patient relationship,
22-24
accepting or declining patients,
58-59
billing, 59-60
boundary violations. See
Boundary violations
confidentiality. See
Confidentiality
Consent. See Consent
coverage, 55-56, 64-65
duty to warn. See Duty to warn
evaluative relationships, 24
fiduciary duty, 23, 44, 65-66

litigious patients, 61-63
overdue accounts, 60-61
professional style and avoiding
lawsuits, 64
"special relationship," 22-23
suicide. See Suicide
termination of care, 34-35, 60-
61, 66-68, 143
variation in duty related to type
of, 40-41
Colleagues, impaired or unethical,
121-128
Colleague's practice, covering, 40
Collection agencies, 60
Commit, duty to, 116
Communication, 62
Competence:
as element of consent, 75
to stand trial, 19-20
Complaint, 141-142
Confidentiality, 13n, 45, 91-98
common misunderstandings, 97-
98
disclosure to payers, 98
duty to warn. See Duty to warn
exchanging information with
other professionals, 91-92
getting information from others,
93-94
giving information to family
members, 92-93
impaired or unethical colleagues
and, 123, 125-126
release of information, 94-96
rural or isolated practice settings and, 71
subpoenas, 96

suicide and, 106-107
Conflict of interest, 23
  financial, 66
  rural or isolated practice set-
    tings and, 71
Consent, 11, 26-28, 64, 75-79
  advance directives, 79
  assent, 78
  elements of, 75-76
  expiration of, 78
  expressed, 78
  implied, 77-78
  informed, 76-77
  release of information, 94-96
  to release patient information.
    See Confidentiality; Privilege
  specificity of, 27-28
  written vs. oral, 76
Constitutional rights, 29
Constitution of the United States,
  16, 17
Constitutions, state, 16, 29
Consultants, expert, 18-19, 135-
  136, 144
Consultation, 9-10, 53-55
  adverse effects of treatment and,
    132
  clinical, defined, 40
  duty to warn and, 115,
    119-120
  litigious patients and, 62-63
  by telephone, 40
Content of release authorizations,
  95
Continuing education, 8
Contractor instructions, 35
Contracts, clinical, 43-46

Controversial subspecialties, 72
Correctional system, patients in,
  21-22
Co-treatment, 9, 10, 55-56
Countertransference vulnerability,
  6-7
Courts, 16, 19
Coverage, 55-56, 64-65
Credentials, 5-6
Criminal law, 19-22
Criminal matters, burden of proof
  and, 17
Criminal responsibility, 20-21
Crisis settings, 40, 64

Damage, 25
Dangerousness assessment,
  109-111
  See also Duty to warn
Declining patients, 32, 58-59
Denying care for financial
  reasons, 34-35
Depositions, 144-145
Diagnosis:
  financial limitations and,
    33-34
  inappropriate, 87-88
Directives, advance, 79
Disability agencies, 137
Disclosure, 13
  See also Confidentiality
Discretionary activities, 46
Dissociative identity disorders, 28
Divided treatment, 9, 10
Documentation, 12-13
Donations, 89
Dual agency, 21n, 44

Duties of clinicians, 22-24
Duty to care, 31
Duty to commit, 116
Duty to warn, 108-120
  discharge of, 113-116
  help from lawyers and profes-
    sional organizations, 119-120
  identity of potential victims,
    113
  as state-by-state matter, 111
  substance-abuse patients and,
    118-119
  Tarasoff decision, 17, 108-109
  thresholds for "reason to sus-
    pect real danger," 111-112
  timing of, 111
  warning potential victims, 114-
    115, 117-118

Emergency settings, 40, 64
Employer instructions, 35
Employer or employee relation-
  ship, 46-50
Employer references, 56-57
Ethical guidelines, 7, 25
Evaluations, forensic, 136-138
Evaluative relationships, 24
Expert witnesses or consultants,
  18-19, 135-136, 144
Expressed consent, 26-27, 78

Facts, in legal system, 18-19
Fact testimony, 18
Family members:
  contact with, 13-14
  giving information to, 92-93

suicide and, 102-104
Federal laws, 16
Fiduciary duty, 23, 44, 65-66
Financial conflict of interest, 66
Financial gains beyond reasonable
  fee or exchange, 88-89
Financial limitations, 31-35
Forensic training and practice,
  133-138
Forms, 155-166
Fraudulent billing, 59
Friendship, 11

Gifts, 88-89
Good-faith reporting, 121-128
Government agencies, 16
Guidelines *vs.* clinical standards of
  care, 38-39
Gutheil, Thomas, 53, 91n

Historical information, obtaining,
  93-94

Illegal representation, 38
Impaired therapists, 14
Implied consent, 77-78
Independent contractor, 43-46
Information, release of, 94-96
  See also Confidentiality
Informed consent, 76-77
Insanity, 21
"Inside information," 89-90
Instructions from employers or
  contractors, 35
Insurance carrier notification, 142
Interrogatories, 144

Isolated practice settings, 71-72
Isolation, intellectual and professional, 9-10

Joint liability, 10
Journals, 186
Judges, 19
Juries, 19
Jurisdiction, 16-17

Knowledge, 75

Law enforcement agencies, notification of, 114
Lawsuits. *See* Malpractice actions
Lawyers:
  duty to warn and consultation with, 119-120
  forensic cases and, 133-136
  malpractice actions and, 139-145
Least restrictive clinically appropriate alternative, 41-42
Legal system, 15-30
  adversarial system, 17
  burden of proof, 17-18
  competence, 19-20
  consent, 26-28
  criminal responsibility, 20-21
  duties of clinicians, 22-24
  ethical guidelines and, 25
  facts, 18-19
  federal laws, 16
  jurisdiction, 16-17
  negligence and malpractice, 25-26

patients involved with criminal justice system, 21
  patients' rights, 29-30
  permissive nature of, 15-16
  standard of care, 24-25
  state laws, 16, 28-29
Legal terms, glossary of, 167-185
Letters of reference or recommendation, 126-128
License to practice, 23, 44
Licensing boards, 121, 123-126
Litigious patients, 61-63
Local laws, 16
Locations, session, 85-86

Malpractice actions, 139-146
  appeals, 146
  complaint or petition, 141-142
  conditions for malpractice, 25-26
  defense lawyer, 140-141
  depositions, 144-145
  expert witnesses or consultants, 144
  helping the defense lawyer, 142-143
  insurance carrier notification, 142
  interrogatories, 144
  notification of, 139-140
  settlement, 145
  termination of care and, 143
  trials, 145
Malpractice liability, 38
Managed care, 70
Medicare, 98n

Minors' records, 92-93
Misunderstandable subspecialties, 72
Moral guidelines, 7-8

National Association of Social Workers, 7
National Practitioner Data Bank, 25
Negligence, 25-26
Negligence lawsuits, 42
Nonpayment, terminating treatment for, 60-61
Notes, 12-13, 105

Office hours, 85-86
On-call professionals, 64-65
Oral consent, 76
Overdue accounts, 60-61

Patient-clinician relationship. See Clinician-patient relationship
Patient requests vs. standard of care, 36-37
Patients' Bill of Rights, 30, 69n
Patients' rights, 29-30, 41, 42, 69n
Payers, disclosure to, 98
Permissive nature of legal system, 15-16
Petition, 141-142
Physically ill colleagues, 124
Policies vs. clinical standards of care, 38-39
Practice settings and styles, 69-74
  managed care, 70
  rural or isolated, 71-72
  unusual, controversial, or easily

misunderstandable subspecialties, 72
Precertification review, 33
President of the United States, threats against, 113
Privilege, 91
  See also Confidentiality
Professional organizations, 25, 119-120, 123
Professional references, 56-57
Professional relationships, 43-68
  clinician-patient. See Clinician-patient relationship
  consultant, 53-55
  co-treater, 55-56
  employer or employee, 46-50
  independent contractor, 43-46
  professional or employer references, 56-57, 126-128
  therapist supervisor, 50-53
Professional style, 64
Promises, 39-40
Prospective release, 95-96
Protect, duty to. See Duty to warn
Psychiatric screening, 38
Psychiatry, 38
Psychological autopsies, 105-106
Psychology, 38
Psychotherapy, 38

Qualifications, proof of, 44-45

Reasonable care, duty to exercise, 46-47
Recommendation, letters of, 126-128
Recording therapy sessions, 84-85

Records:
dishonest, 87-88
release of. *See* Confidentiality
suicide and, 106-107
"Red flags," 83-84
References, professional or
employer, 56-57, 126-128
Referrals, 91-92
Reid/Zeig, Tucker National Survey
on Forensic Issues in the Mental
Health Professions, 147-154
Release of information, 94-96
Reporting impaired or unethical
colleagues, 121-128
Reports, dishonest, 87-88
Repressed memories, 28
Reputation, 14
Resources, 186-188
Respondeat superior, 46, 49, 50
Right to treatment, 29
Rural practice, 71-72

Schlesinger, Laura, 7
Search warrants, 106-107
Self-serving notes, 105
Senior citizens, confidentiality
protections for, 98*n*
Sentencing, patients awaiting, 21
Settlement, 145
Sexual boundary violations, 80-87
avoiding opportunity for
accusations, 83-85
locations and, 85-86
office hours and, 85-86
responsibility for reporting,
86-87
Shakespeare, William, 14

Side effects of treatment, 129
Social pressure *vs.* standard of
care, 36-37
"Special relationship," 22-24
Specialty, practicing beyond, 37-38
Standards of care. *See* Clinical
standards of care
State laws, 16, 28-29
Style, professional, 64
Subpoenas, 96, 107
Substance-abusing patients,
118-119
Substance-abusing professionals,
124
Substitute therapists, 55-56
Suicide, 99-107
assessment, 100
awareness, 99
protecting the patient, 100-102
responses to, 102-107
Sullivan, Harry Stack, 88
Supervision, 8-10, 50-53
Szasz, Thomas, 5

Tarasoff vs. The Regents of The
University of California, 17,
108-109
Telephone, consultation by, 40-41
Termination of care, 34-35, 60-61,
66-68, 143
Testimony, 137
Therapeutic correctness, 10-11
Therapist supervisor, 50-53
Third-party contracts, 44, 45
"Topic-limited" supervision, 52
Touching, 83
Training, 5-6, 37-38

Treatment, adverse effects of,
    129-132
Triage, 40
Trials:
    malpractice action, 145
    patients awaiting, 21

Unusual subspecialties, 72
U.S. Secret Service, 113
U.S. Supreme Court, 16, 29
Utilization review, 33

Victims, potential:
    identity of, 113
    warning, 114-115, 117-118
Voluntariness, 75-76

Warn, duty to. *See* Duty to warn
Web sites, 187-188
Witnesses, expert, 18-19, 135-136,
    144
Written consent, 76